THE **1%**
PRINCIPLE

THE 1% PRINCIPLE

TOM O'NEIL

HarperCollins*Publishers*

HarperCollins*Publishers*

First published in 2013
by HarperCollins*Publishers (New Zealand) Limited*
PO Box 1, Shortland Street, Auckland 1140

HarperCollins*Publishers*
31 View Road, Glenfield, Auckland 0627, New Zealand
Level 13, 201 Elizabeth Street, Sydney, NSW 2000, Australia
A 53, Sector 57, Noida, UP, India
77–85 Fulham Palace Road, London W6 8JB, United Kingdom
2 Bloor Street East, 20th floor, Toronto, Ontario M4W 1A8, Canada
10 East 53rd Street, New York, NY 10022, USA

National Library of New Zealand Cataloguing-in-Publication Data
O'Neil, Tom, 1971-
The 1% principle / Tom O'Neil.
ISBN 978-1-77554-023-6
1. Success. 2. Change (Psychology).
3. Self-actualization (Psychology).
I. Title.
158.1—dc 23

ISBN: 978 1 77554 023 6

Cover design by Cheryl Rowe
Cover image by Cary Johnson
Typesetting by IslandBridge

Printed by Griffin Press, Australia

The papers used by HarperCollins in the manufacture of
this book are a natural, recyclable product made from wood
grown in sustainable plantation forests. The fibre source
and manufacturing processes meet recognised international
environmental standards, and carry certification.

Contents

Part Two: Examples of the 1% Principle in your life, work and business

Part Three: Use the 30 Day Programme to successfully implement the 1% Principle in your life, work and business

Part One

The 1% Principle

Small incremental steps, practised over time
and consistently focused towards a specific goal,
can't help but bring your dreams to reality.

What is the 1% Principle?

Most business and self-development books make a promise of secret wisdom on the cover, yet only reveal their key points a couple of hundred pages into the book. *The 1% Principle* is different. This book will immediately give you the key to massively increasing your business and personal success, then spend the rest of the book explaining how to implement these principles in a real-world way.

Unfortunately, most people think self-improvement and life planning is something only people who own Ferraris do. The vast majority of people spend far more time planning their wedding day or buying a second-hand car than they do planning their life and their career.

This is why fewer than one in 30 people invest in motivational books and programmes and actively plan their lives through formal goal setting. On a positive note, you are probably one of these people as you are reading these words right now!

The 1% Principle focuses on making the transition to a better and more productive life a lot easier. Achieving lots of 'mini-goals' over a short to medium period, you can quickly transform what you achieve and how you want to live.

The entire philosophy is very simple. It is based around asking the following questions:

- ▶ **Me** 'The 1% Principle — What is one thing I can do today to improve my life by 1%?'
- ▶ **My community** 'The 1% Principle — What is one thing I can do today to improve the life of someone near me by 1%?'

Unlike a formal goal programme, the 1% Principle is more of a life philosophy, rather than a tool or resource you draw upon during a set time. As you become more successful using this principle, you will start to reflect on it more and more as you begin to see positive changes in key areas of your life. Over time, it will become an inbuilt and automatic way of thinking, helping you to reach further in your life, without being fully conscious of the effort required.

The butterfly effect

In 1961, American mathematician and meteorologist Edward Lorenz was using a numerical formula to assess a weather model, when, as a short cut, he entered the decimal 0.506 instead of 0.506127. The result was a completely unexpected and quite different weather scenario from what was initially predicted.

From this experience Lorenz coined the term 'butterfly effect', whereby small changes in an environment (such as the flap of a butterfly's wings) can have major consequences (a tornado in Texas).

The butterfly effect has its roots in chaos theory and is very similar to the 1% Principle, as it reinforces the fact that small initial changes of seemingly minor significance can set the scene for major transformation.

For example, a decision I personally made to get fit and lose some excess weight a number of years ago led me to start jogging. Six months later, this led to my first competitive (albeit slow) run. This in turn saw me one year later complete the Oxfam Trailwalker, successfully walking 100 kilometres in under 24 hours.

Little initial decisions and challenges successfully overcome build a foundation to let you go to the next stage. At that next stage, new and potentially unforeseen opportunities open up, which help you to rise even further in your personal development very quickly.

Why is goal setting so important?

We set goals many times every day. Whether it's to make the bus on time to work, to catch up with some friends or to go to do some digging in the garden, we tend not to think about these as goals as they are just part of 'what we do' to have a functional life.

We have all been told throughout our lives how important it is to set goals; however, the stark fact is that fewer than 5% of people have formal written goals that they regularly update and manage as they go through their life.

A popular story, cited by many motivational leaders, recalls a Yale University study that took place in 1953. Researchers interested in studying goal setting surveyed the graduating seniors from Yale University about their goals and aspirations for the future. They discovered that only 3% of the graduating class had detailed, written goals. When they tracked down the same graduates in 1973, the researchers were amazed at the results. They discovered that the same 3% who had clearly written goals when they graduated in 1953 were more successful, and worth more in terms of wealth, than the other 97% put together.

Sadly, while this study is widely cited by hundreds of very reputable sources, it seems this research never happened. Instead, a similar inspirational study took place, led by Dr Gail Matthews, at the Dominican University of California. The study provided practical evidence of the effectiveness of three coaching tools: accountability, commitment and writing down one's goals. The study also found that those who wrote their goals achieved significantly more than those who did not write down their goals.

All too hard ...

The unfortunate reality is that most people spend more time planning their vacation than planning their lives. Statistics show that the average American spends more than four hours a day watching TV or surfing the web.

> 'Cheshire Puss,' she began, rather timidly, as she did not at all know whether it would like the name: however, it only grinned a little wider. 'Come, it's pleased so far,' thought Alice, and she went on. 'Would you tell me, please, which way I ought to go from here?'
>
> 'That depends a good deal on where you want to get to,' said the Cat.
>
> 'I don't much care where—' said Alice.
>
> 'Then it doesn't matter which way you go,' said the Cat.
>
> '—so long as I get SOMEWHERE,' Alice added as an explanation.
>
> 'Oh, you're sure to do that,' said the Cat, 'if you only walk long enough.'
>
> —Lewis Carroll, *Alice's Adventures in Wonderland*

It is a common philosophy among many people today that as long as they have some motion or perceived progress, they are okay. This only works, however, if you are aiming towards a goal you want to achieve.

Big steps towards nothing get you nowhere!

On the other hand, small incremental steps, practised over time and consistently focused towards a specific goal, can't help but bring that goal to reality at some stage.

Your life as a single choice

A life of 80 years is broken into 29,200 days, which equates to more than 700,000 hours or 42 million minutes. Over a person's life they make tens of millions of choices. However, the next decision they make will be the important one, as all future choices will be based on that next decision.

What are mini-goals?

A mini-goal is usually (though not always) a specific decision and action you take to immediately improve something in your own or someone else's life. They are not necessarily major life-changing actions, but when they are all added up towards a specific objective they can have a massive impact on your productivity and quality of life.

Examples of mini-goals include:

▶ Phoning a family member you may have lost touch with just to say hi.

▶ Disciplining yourself to not have fizzy drinks (soda) or fast food for five days.

▶ Going for two 10-minute walks twice this week.

▶ Committing to spend 20 minutes finishing off an unpleasant project at work or home that has been dragging on for weeks.

▶ Buying fresh ingredients and cooking a meal for you and your family.

▶ Phoning up about that salsa class you are interested in.

As you become comfortable with setting and achieving regular mini-goals, you may want to develop more structure and link these mini-goals to larger short-, medium- and long-term goals. This will give you a definite purpose and vision for the future. My COMPASS Goal Achievement Programme, detailed later in this book, gives you a way to do this in a tangible and easily accessible way, making mini-goals a small part of your grand plan.

The power of mini-goals

Mini goals are excellent for the following reasons:

Mini-goals are achievable

Mini-goals are very achievable and give you a real sense of success. Most people fail when they set their goals as the goals are too large and they get discouraged when they don't reach their targets.

For example, if you wish to lose some excess weight, having a mini-goal of losing (and keeping off) 1 kilogram over two weeks is something that can be achieved with a small amount of discipline. On the other hand, saying that you will commit to losing 4 kilograms in two weeks will involve a lot of stress during the process and disappointment if you fail. Also, the shorter term mini-goal is more sustainable and in the long term will provide a firm foundation for future weight loss.

Mini-goals give purpose and focus

When you achieve your first mini-goal, this encourages you to make mini-goals a pattern, then a lifestyle. This encouragement gives you focus and drive to achieve more challenging targets, leading to more feelings of self-worth and a higher level of success in your family, career and spiritual life.

When I was young, I was told I needed to pray every day for one hour to be effective in my faith. However, when on the fourth day I did not manage to do this, I condemned myself, which then led to feelings of failure. This led to me giving up on my prayer and study times altogether at that stage of my life.

Soon after, a good friend of mine, Pastor Aaron Roberts, advised me to commit to praying for only two minutes a day. When he said this to me I thought, 'What sort of person only prays for two minutes a day?' However, I tried it, found it easy, increased the time period gradually and made it a 'locked-in' lifestyle choice. I have now been doing this for almost 20 years.

One major aspect of this story for me is patience. We are conditioned to want and get things now! Easy credit and a lifestyle of consumption and disposable goods feed this insatiable need to want and get more, sometimes at the expense of our long-term credit history.

Mini-goals are excellent as they give you an instant feeling of gratification, and cumulatively over time make a huge difference to your quality of life.

Mini-goals supercharge your journey

Mini-goals give you the 'fuel' to take real steps towards your short-, medium- and long-term future. When you start to succeed in specific areas in your life, you become more aware of your potential and what you can actually achieve if you put your mind to it.

Of course, if you look to improve your life by 1% over 100 days, the results can be extraordinary.

> 'We are what we repeatedly do. Excellence, therefore, is not an act but a habit.'
> —Aristotle

Tweaking your way to success ...

If we actively look to just adjust or tweak our lives by 1% a day, we can quickly make great progress today towards who we want to be tomorrow.

For example, stopping smoking is a big goal, but if you make a mini-goal of smoking three fewer cigarettes a day, this equals one pack fewer you smoke a week. This in turn becomes 52 packs a year, which equates to more than $1000 saved in gross wages. If you earn $40,000 a year, you have saved 3% of your taxable income from slightly reducing smoking ...

Over time, make another mini-goal of another three fewer

cigarettes, until you gradually stop. That's it! Nice and simple: 'What can you do today to make your life 1% better?'

> 'Every day do something that will inch you closer
> to a better tomorrow.'
>
> —Doug Firebaugh, author, trainer, international speaker

'Little short-term change

=

big long-term change.'

—Chris Knox, business and thought leader

Why we fail in
our goals

Everyone has failures throughout their life and this is a natural part of being human. However, life is not measured by how many times you fall; it's measured by how many times you get back up again.

> 'Success is not final, failure is not fatal: it is the courage to continue that counts.'
> —Winston Churchill

If you fail and get discouraged with a particular goal, there is a wide range of reasons why this could have happened. Common themes include the following:

Trying too much too quickly

Traditionally, when people set goals they get excited, then set up a whole range of targets that are poorly thought out, both in regards to the resources available (including time and money) and time frame. This then means they start to miss deadlines and the progress towards their goals begins to fall away. After a couple of key progress milestones pass, they say to themselves, 'This is too hard. I cannot set and achieve my goals — I am a failure at this.'

Sadly, a common problem is that when people set their short-, medium- and long-term life goals, their short-term goals are too aggressive and they set themselves up for failure right from the start. However, this is where the 1% Principle is so valuable.

Because the entire approach is based on small steps, this system helps minimise the risk that you won't achieve your goals, as you are taking a day-by-day focus towards their fruition.

No passion for the goal

I recently ran my COMPASS Goal Achievement Programme for a group of CEOs and business leaders. Halfway through the morning, one of the group stopped me in mid-sentence, saying, 'I don't like this session with you, Tom!'

With my heart in my mouth I asked what was wrong. 'Nothing,' he replied. 'Except you have just made me realise that for my whole life I have been living other people's goals they have set for me! I have never stopped and thought about what I want for my life.'

This came as a true revelation for this man, who on the outside looked every part the successful senior executive. However, he was living how other people thought he should live, and was not being true to himself.

In another example, family psychologist Dr James Dobson talks about a man whose father and grandfather were both surgeons. No prizes for guessing what the family expected the man to do for a vocation when he developed into adulthood. This person dutifully studied and became qualified as a doctor, then completed further study to become a surgeon. His family of course was very proud, and he developed a successful career. However, the day his father died, the man resigned from his post at a leading hospital and signed up for a new job as a builder's labourer. His personal passion had always been for building and construction and he had no real joy or passion for the medical profession.

It sounds basic, but ensure that the goals you set are *your* goals — not goals set by your parents, friends, guidance counsellors or university professors. Be true to who you are and who you want to be.

Procrastination/distraction

The ability to procrastinate and get distracted by a wide range of unimportant things can be very strong, especially when the next stage of your goal is some distance away. Tasks such as tidying your desk or cleaning your car take on a new importance. This becomes a trap because we unwisely devote our time to these small jobs, then get caught when it becomes apparent that we cannot reach our goals in time.

Remember to always look forward and make a 1% step towards your goals every day. Every little step counts.

Discouragement when we fail/fear of failure

A lot of the time we don't achieve our goals because we are afraid that we may be seen as a fraud or a failure if things don't go according to plan. This leads to a state of 'development paralysis', whereby we don't strive towards the goals we set, then later on don't set any goals at all.

Don't worry what other people think; just focus on taking that next 1% step towards your destiny. Making an attempt is what really counts.

> 'It is not the critic who counts; not the man who points out how the strong man stumbles, or where the doer of deeds could have done them better. The credit belongs to the man who is actually in the arena, whose face is marred by dust and sweat and blood, who strives valiantly; who errs and comes short again and again …'
> —Theodore Roosevelt

P
A
R
T

O
N
E

> '*Small deeds done are better than great deeds planned.*'

—Peter Marshall, philosopher and historian

Getting there with mini-goals

'Obstacles are those frightful things you see when you
take your eyes off your goal.'
—Henry Ford

The opportunity to massively transform your life within a short
time frame is possible with mini-goals. As mentioned earlier, little
short-term changes equate to big long-term changes.

What does having a life that is gradually changed for good
look like? What are the daily habits I need and the principles I
need to know to be effective in doing this?

The great part of mini-goals is that your first 'trial' goal can be
really easy. For example, rounding up all the overdue DVDs in your
house and returning them to the shop so you don't incur late fees.
The next day your mini-goal may be to go for a small walk for 10
minutes. No jogging, no sweatpants, no spandex. Just comfortable
shoes and you. Day three may involve you phoning your insurance
agent to confirm your health policy that was waylaid.

No matter what the goal, you are just after a small positive
change in your circumstances (or someone else's) that will make
a 1% difference that day. The principle of this change is that, after
100 days, you start to have a greatly improved life with improved
relationships, financial security and better health. This flows into a
healthier state of mind with you feeling more confident about the
future. An improved mindset allows you to better deal with stress
and pressure, leading to a longer and more fulfilled life.

It's the small successes that keep you consistently motivated.

'Seventy per cent of success in life
is showing up.'

—Woody Allen

The eight key laws of the 1% Principle

The 1% Principle is governed by eight key laws that will assist you in making the most of this system. Being aware of and applying these laws will help you to more effectively leverage your small decisions, allowing them to have a large ongoing impact.

Remember, however, that quality change takes time.

> 'You have to put in many, many, many tiny efforts that nobody sees or appreciates before you achieve anything worthwhile.'
>
> —Brian Tracy, author, international speaker

Law One:
The Law of the Small

Small things tend to be neglected by society in general, but as many people know, 'if you take care of the little things, the big things will look after themselves'.

Most of our decisions and actions are small and take place within a few seconds. However, one decision made in an instant can echo throughout eternity in a positive or negative way.

An example of something small that significantly changed history is the humble flea. In AD 542, fleas carrying the plague arrived in Constantinople, working their way through the Byzantine Empire, then into Rome. The epidemic is estimated to have killed approximately 25 million people in the Roman Empire alone. This was even before the more famous 'Black Death', which reduced the entire world's population from around 450 million to around 360 million in the fourteenth century.

Another example of the small things making a big difference was the 1989 Tour de France. This race took place over 23 days, passed through both the Pyrenees and the Alps, and overall spanned more than 3285 kilometres (2041 miles). Competition was tight between the two main rivals Greg LeMond (USA) and Laurent Fignon (France). Going into the final stage, LeMond was trailing Fignon by 50 seconds. However, LeMond completed the stage 58 seconds faster than Fignon, and claimed the title.

What is amazing is that eight seconds at the professional level is one slip of the pedal, braking slightly too much around a corner, or not quite pushing as hard as you can up a small incline. This tiny amount of effort expended was the difference between second and champion, over a total distance from California to Florida or from London to 700 kilometres past Moscow ...

Some racing specialists believe that due to LeMond wearing an advanced aerodynamic helmet, and Fignon having his head bare and letting his ponytail flail around in the wind, LeMond gained 16 seconds in the last stage. Who would ever have thought that a haircut would determine the winner of the Tour de France?

In the political world, small things have time and again made a huge impact on the world stage. The 2000 US election was a titanic struggle between Republican candidate George W Bush and Democratic candidate Vice President Al Gore. As voting drew to a close, all eyes were focused on Florida, where through a complex electoral model, winning this key state meant winning the overall election. Finally, when the dust and legal challenges had settled, Bush had won Florida by 537 votes and became the next President of the USA. In regards to mathematic ratios, Bush won Florida by 0.0092%. Just 538 people voting differently, out of a total of over 19 million across the state, could have made a completely different outcome to not just American policy, but the world as a whole. (To make matters even stranger, Al Gore won the total election across America by more than 540,000 votes, although the complex state-based system meant he actually lost overall.)

The lesson is: small is important. Small is king!

Law Two:
The Law of Cumulative Effect

Imagine a snowball rolling down a hill. Initially, a tiny amount of energy is transferred to form a small ball of ice. Over time, slightly more mass and energy build up, allowing the snowball to move forward slowly, by force of gravity. As it turns, it gains more mass, and also gains more momentum, allowing it to move faster down the hill. For each full revolution of the snowball, more snow is added, generating over the period of a few seconds a large moving object that is very difficult to stop!

In many ways, the 1% Principle operates just like this. Each small and positive decision in a specific area allows the 'snowball' to quickly grow, resulting in this area of your life moving ahead quickly.

I firmly believe having a successful life is a very simple process. The more wise and positive choices you make, the more successful you will be. For example, if you make 1000 positive choices for every one negative or destructive choice, the numbers will invariably lead to a positive outcome. Conversely, if you make 100 positive choices for every one negative or destructive choice, the negative consequences will accumulate 10 times faster, leading to more challenges in your life.

Each choice you make invariably leads to another set of decisions based on that previous choice. The more good choices you make, the more your path will ascend, allowing you to reach your potential.

In a letter from the famous scientist Sir Isaac Newton to his friend Robert Hooke, Newton describes how his scientific success was built on the knowledge and hard work of those that had gone before him: 'If I have seen further, it is by standing on the shoulders of giants.'

There is a similar theme in the 1% Principle, whereby you stand (or fall) based on the wise (or not) decisions you have made right up until this moment in your life.

A traditional Indian legend highlighting the Law of Cumulative Effect talks about a king whose great passion was to challenge visitors to a game of chess. On one occasion a wise traveller was told by the king that he could name his price if he won. The traveller thought for a while and then named his price: the king was to put a single grain of rice on the first chess square and double it on every square thereafter. The maths-challenged king thought this was a great idea and quickly accepted. However, after losing, he realised that this method meant he owed the traveller 18,446,744,073,709,551,615 grains of rice — a pile of rice larger than Mt Everest!

Good and bad choices are cumulative. Bad choices also have the power to limit your potential very quickly. Deciding to have a 'toke' of marijuana on a beach, then getting caught by the police and prosecuted, will see you get a criminal conviction. This in turn will mean you cannot travel to some destinations overseas for a holiday and you may also miss out on a variety of job opportunities to further develop your career (not to mention your finances). In some countries, this particular choice leads to even harsher penalties — a very negative outcome!

Other not so dramatic but certainly negative choices are prevalent in our diet. In today's fast food and fizzy drink (soda) culture, the decision to have French fries instead of an apple may not seem a big deal. However, multiply the calories of those French fries (360 calories in a medium-sized 135 gram serving) every day over 10 years (1,314,871 calories), versus an apple

(72 calories) every day for 10 years (262,974), and the difference is staggering!

Considering you burn around 400 calories for every one hour of light jogging, you would need to run for 3287 hours (that's 273 12-hour days) to burn off all those fries, otherwise they go straight to your hips! Put another way, that's like jogging all the way from London to Singapore. Then back again …

Drink a 350 ml (12 oz) can of Coke (43 calories per 100 ml) every day for 10 years, and you have consumed 549,719 calories. Compare this to 10 years drinking a 350 ml glass of water (zero calories), and the difference is clear.

The cumulative effect of ongoing poor diet choices over your life will lead to diabetes, heart problems and general poor health. Good daily choices, on the other hand, will most probably give you another 20 to 30 years of full health that you can share with your family.

Law Three:
The Law of Positive and Negative

In many ways there are no neutral choices. A decision (and corresponding action) is either good or bad, and will make your life better or worse, taking you closer to or further from your goals and who you want to be.

> 'If what you are doing is not moving you towards your goals, then it's moving you away from your goals.'
> —Brian Tracy

This approach is fundamental if you want to achieve strong change over the short and medium term.

Brian Tracy shares in his blog a story that highlights this concept. Flying from Los Angeles to Tokyo, he realised that the plane was actually going to be off course from its destination 99%

'Make at least one definite move
daily toward your goal.'

—Bruce Lee

of the time. Due to unforeseen circumstances like updraughts, downdraughts and other weather activity, the pilots were continually making course corrections, ensuring their final destination was Narita Airport in Tokyo.

During the flight, very tiny changes in speed and direction determine where the plane will end up. The 1% Principle is like that: very small and positive tweaks and changes to your lifestyle will see you make great progress towards where you want to be.

The opposite of this is poor choices (both large and small). Poor choices can significantly veer the angle and speed of the aircraft, taking a large amount of fuel to get back on course. In a person's life this fuel equates to things such as passion and energy, which are precious commodities and require constant daily refilling. Therefore, the fewer negative course corrections you make, the less personal energy you will have to spend getting back on track.

Remember, every decision is taking you only towards or further away from your goals. Once you are in the pilot's seat and take over the controls of your life, your goals will start to take on a life of their own. What we start building up will start building us up.

Law Four:
The Law of Gradual Change

The Law of Gradual Change focuses on the fact that we have only a limited amount of time today to make a positive impact in both our own and other people's lives.

Like a glacier moving slowly forward, carving out a valley, your life moves inexorably forward, carving out either a small creek or a canyon. The momentum and impact you make on yourself and those around you is linked directly to the daily small choices you make. Gradual change tends to set in and becomes a way of life, while instant change may only be fleeting and quickly melt away.

Psychology professors Diener, Fujita and Suh from the

University of Illinois found in their 1996 study 'Events and Subjective Well-Being: Only Recent Events Matter' that only recent events impact a person's feeling of well-being. Studying 115 participants over a two-year period, they found only life events that took place within the previous three months influenced overall life satisfaction.

An example of this principle is the fact that many Lotto winners, while thrilled and ecstatic over their initial win of a large amount of money, quickly readjust to normality. In fact, various academic studies show that lottery winners are not happier than people generally, as they take significantly less pleasure from everyday events.

Losing weight is also a good example of this law. Dr Donald Hensrud from the Mayo Clinic writes that 'fast weight loss usually takes extraordinary efforts in diet and exercise — efforts that could be unhealthy and that you probably can't maintain as permanent lifestyle changes'.

While the initial results of rapid weight loss can be positive, as a rule it is not feasible to continue this as an ongoing lifestyle, and old habits and behaviours will take over once you have lost weight. However, a more measured, focused and long-term approach to weight loss will see you make small positive change, at a pace and in a lifestyle you can manage.

The power of the 1% Principle is that you need to make only one genuine improvement today to have some success. The positive outcome here is that when you consistently make positive changes in your life, and start to reap some of the rewards of these choices, you will become more empowered and less tempted to procrastinate.

Small, gradual change is deep and real change. Like a glacier moving slowly down the mountain, our lives will leave an impact on those around us. The depth and influence that this impact will leave (either positive or negative) is dependent on our daily choices, decisions and actions.

Law Five:
The Law of Constant Improvement

As you start to use the 1% Principle in your daily life, you will notice that the small changes you implement will gradually accumulate into some very positive outcomes. This is the Law of Constant Improvement in action.

In business, this principle is known as kaizen, Japanese for 'improvement' or 'change for the better'. The international car maker Toyota used this principle in the manufacturing of their vehicles to tremendous effect. Having made one out of every nine vehicles on the planet in 2011, Toyota focused on kaizen as a way to ensure quality and a strong drive for efficiency in all aspects of production.

Their model is quite simple:

1 Standardise an operation/activity.

2 Measure the operation/activity.

3 Assess measurements against the outcome required.

4 Come up with new, innovative ways to increase efficiency and productivity.

5 Standardise the improved operation.

Focused towards ongoing small improvements in all aspects of the business, this approach yields large results in the form of compound productivity improvement.

Transferring this into a person's life, this format provides a simple way to improve your performance:

1 Assess the key areas of your life.

2 Measure your performance in these areas.

3 Create an innovative way to slightly improve your performance on a daily basis, in one of these areas.

4 Repeat by implementing the 1% Principle every day.

As you make small positive daily choices, you effectively take a 'mini-step' up the ladder to where you want to be. Taking one of these steps every day reinforces your decisions, leading to you becoming more competent in different areas of your life.

Law Six:
The Law of Sowing and Reaping

In the New Testament book of Galatians, the Apostle Paul states, 'What a person plants, he will harvest.' This holds very true for the 1% Principle. As you invest yourself into a particular task or skill, your opportunity to develop this ability improves. This leads to more opportunities you may not have been aware of, leading to greater personal growth.

For example, recently I got published in the *Harvard Business Review* blog. After a year of reading the odd *HBR* article on LinkedIn, I stumbled across a post asking for specialists in the careers and personal development area to provide content. I immediately contacted the editor, pitched my article idea and then got the opportunity to write and be featured in the *Harvard Business Review*. I then leveraged this article by contacting *The Economist* magazine, pitching a new idea using the recent *HBR* article as a means of building my credibility. This then led to me being published and having my own Q&A forum for a week on *The Economist* website.

As fantastic as this was, I was then asked by *The Economist* to be the keynote speaker at their international careers fair. A week after I spoke at their event, Harvard Publishing contacted me to ask if I would be happy to contribute a section for a careers and personal development guide they were writing.

This is where the 1% Principle can really operate well. From an initial decision to contact the *Harvard Business Review* then *The Economist*, without any effort on my part, I gained further recognition around the world as an expert promoted by *The*

Economist as well as getting published by one of the world's leading universities.

When you continually sow positive change in your life, the 1% Principle turbo-charges your performance, helping you reap the rewards and reach the next level faster.

Law Seven:
The Law of the Decision and Action

> 'In any moment of decision, the best thing you can do is
> the right thing, the next best thing is the wrong thing,
> and the worst thing you can do is nothing.'
> —Theodore Roosevelt

Nothing happens without a decision and a corresponding action. Most people fail in reaching their potential due to the fact that they just don't make a decision and follow it through.

While a giant goal cannot easily be comprehended, small bites will ensure the goal firstly comes into focus, then reaches completion. Each small bite is a decision and action or, put another way, 'cause and effect'. The cause is your decision to make change; the effect is the following action and the changes it makes in both you and the environment around you.

No matter how big or small your goals are you can always see ahead far enough to take that next step. By deciding on and taking small, well-measured steps, one at a time, you will eventually arrive at your destination, no matter how far away it may seem today.

Law Eight:
The Law of the Paradox

> 'To live a lot, you must die a little.'
> —Robert Lewis (from the DVD series *Authentic Manhood: Winning at Work and Home*)

All goal setting is undergirded by sacrifice. To gain something tomorrow, you must give up something today.

Dr Robert Lewis, author of the Winning at Work and Home personal development series, popularised the 'Paradox Principle' as a way of demonstrating that to achieve your long-term goals, you must make small sacrifices today. The three-word synopsis of the Paradox Principle is 'Die to Live'. While, of course, this seems counter-intuitive, its foundation is key to all short-, medium- and long-term goal setting.

We're faced with countless opportunities every day to choose between a short-term action to fulfil a craving (like buying another cappuccino on the way home from work) or staying the course towards a long-term goal (buying a boat).

Success in any aspect of life demands and requires a cost that must be paid first. That cost is giving up something right now — time, money, prestige or comfort. To invest in your future and the future of others, you sometimes need to do some hard, unselfish and fearful things today, so you can reach your goals tomorrow.

'A journey of a thousand miles
begins with a single step.'

—Laozi, Chinese philosopher

Real-life examples of the 1% Principle at work

1971 Italian Grand Prix

As the driver's championship had already been won, the 1971 Italian Grand Prix at Monza was an opportunity for new drivers to demonstrate their skills. New Zealander Chris Amon in the Matra team aggressively seized pole position at Ferrari's home track, with the BRM team on the second row. Once the race got under way, Clay Regazzoni's Ferrari quickly surged from the fourth row to lead the race.

As the battle progressed, two packs emerged. Coming into the final lap, six drivers were all in striking distance of victory. In fourth place at the last turn, Peter Gethin (a relatively unknown driver from the UK) made an aggressive passing manoeuvre, zooming past the rest of the F1 cars and claiming the chequered flag by 0.01 of a second. Considering that the blink of an eye takes place in 0.4 of a second, the margin of victory was minuscule! Another amazing fact about this race is the difference between first and fifth was 0.61 of a second. One and a half times the blink of an eye …

The Monza 1971 race was for a number of years the fastest Formula One race of all time, recording an average speed of 242 km/h (150 mph). This stunning record went unbroken for another 32 years until the 2003 Italian Grand Prix, again based at Monza.

The key significance of this story is that the little (and I mean tiny) things matter. Over a total race of 316 kilometres (196 miles), a small tap on the brakes too hard coming into a corner, not accelerating quickly enough into a straight section, or the wing mirrors just slightly out of alignment disrupting the car's airflow, meant the difference between coming fifth, or having the title of 'F1 race winner' for the rest of your life.

When competition is very strong, the small things become the big things.

'Dropping the ball'

There are countless examples in sport where a split-second moment of inattention can cost a team the game, the series and the championship.

In the world of international cricket, 28 One Day International games have been won by just one run. At the top of the leader board for bringing home nail-biting wins is:

- ▶ Australia, five occasions
- ▶ New Zealand, four occasions
- ▶ India, four occasions
- ▶ West Indies, three occasions
- ▶ South Africa, three occasions

In one-day cricket each team has 50 six-ball overs, equalling 300 deliveries. However, if you bowl a ball badly (too wide or from too far down the wicket, for example), you are penalised a run and must make the delivery again.

In the May 2011 game between the West Indies and Pakistan at Kensington Oval in Barbados, Pakistani fast bowler Junaid Khan lost discipline for a split second and delivered a wide ball. Later in the game another speedster, Tanvir Ahmed, bowled an illegal 'no ball'. Both infractions cost Pakistan one run each. But these two split-second and undisciplined moments led to the loss against the West Indies on their home ground.

If any sport is an example of the 1% Principle at work, it must be golf. Golf is the most individual sport you can play, with no 'direct' competition other than the pressure of the other players' scores.

At the 2011 Masters Tournament in Augusta, Georgia, Rory McIlroy led the pack from the start, shooting a bogey-free 7-under-par 65 in the first round. Leading until halfway through the fourth and final round, and with prize money of US$1.44 million at stake for the winner, McIlroy self-destructed, shooting a last-round 80, taking him from leader to tying for fifteenth place.

Afterwards McIlroy said, 'I lost a lot of confidence with my putting, but I just hit a poor tee shot on 10 and sort of unravelled from there.' Amazing brilliance for almost 90% of the tournament followed by a few things done poorly led to a meltdown of monumental proportions. Sadly, the 2011 Masters Tournament will be remembered for McIlroy's self-destruction, rather than for the eventual winner Charl Schwartzel.

Even the greatest players in the world have had games (or complete series) when the 1% Principle has come into play. In 1984 the legendary basketball star Magic Johnson had just won two MVP awards and his team the LA Lakers were entering their third consecutive championship challenge. Everyone was expecting Johnson to be a game breaker and dominate the court. The little things, however, ended up making the championship series a horror show for him.

With Game 2 tied, he inexplicably dribbled out the clock, before the Lakers lost in overtime. In Game 4 he turned over the ball in the final minute, then missed two free throws in overtime that lost them the game. Finally, in Game 7, with the Lakers trailing by three points in the last minute, Johnson again lost the ball, sealing the championship title for the Celtics. Unfortunately, this turn of events gained this amazing player the (thankfully temporary) nickname of 'Tragic Johnson'.

However, you can make the 1% Principle count, if you are prepared to learn from your mistakes.

> 'I've missed more than 9000 shots in my career. I've lost almost 300 games. Twenty-six times, I've been trusted to take the game-winning shot and missed. I've failed over and over and over again in my life. And that is why I succeed.'
> —Michael Jordan, basketball great

As long as you accumulate what you learn from all the small failures and disappointments, you will be in a better position next time you are trusted to take the game-winning shot.

P
A
R
T

O
N
E

Starting from the start: where are you today?

When people start setting goals and putting their life in order, they tend firstly to focus on what they are seeking, then make up the plan from there. However, to reach a destination, it's vital to know where you are starting from. Consider your starting point: where are you today? Be honest!

The first step is to ask the following questions:

- ▶ What are the key areas of my life?
- ▶ Where am I succeeding and failing in these areas?
- ▶ Where am I starting from today?
- ▶ How in control of my life am I?

It is vital to have a complete understanding of the answers to these questions, as setting your focus without a clear knowledge of where you are starting from can set you up for failure even before you start.

COMPASS Life Clock Exercise

Decide the key areas of your life that are important to you. These are the things in your life that really matter! They can include tangible areas such as 'children', semi-tangible such as 'marriage' and non-tangible such as 'challenges'.

Step One

For this exercise, choose between five and eight key areas of your life. These key areas are what make you a full person. Suggested examples include:

▶ Finances	▶ Self-worth/self-belief
▶ Health	▶ Lifestyle
▶ Career	▶ Fun
▶ Children	▶ Family
▶ Faith	▶ Marriage
▶ Friends	▶ Challenges

My key life areas

1 ....

2 ....

3 ....

4 ....

5 ....

6 ....

7 ....

8 ....

Step Two

Assign each key area to equally distant points around the circle diagram (Diagram 1). Use the worksheet on page 52 to complete the exercise.

Diagram 1

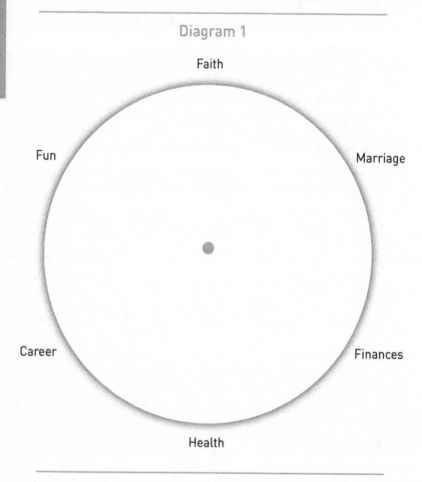

Step Three

Decide how important each key area is to you based on a scale of 1 to 10 (10 = best). Understanding that the point in the centre is zero and the circle is 10, draw a line from the centre to the key area decided for each point. You have now graphically highlighted your key values in your life (Diagram 2).

Diagram 2

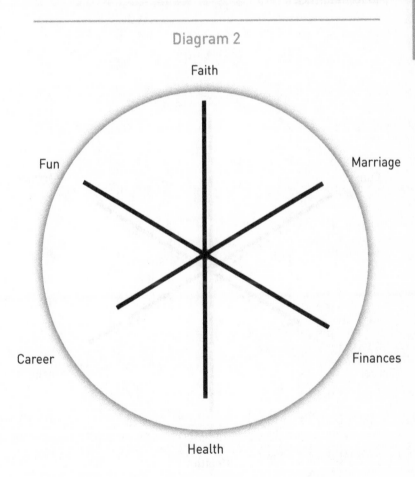

Step Four

Think about each value and determine how you feel you measure up in each of these areas; that is, how successful you feel you are in this area. Draw a second line beside each original line to show this value out of 10 (the dotted line on Diagram 3).

You now see what's important in your life and where you need to focus further.

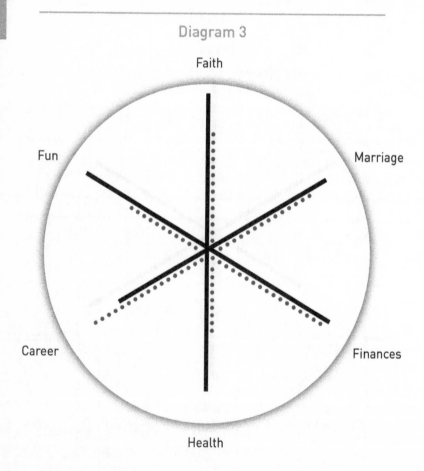

Diagram 3

Step Five

Draw a circle between the points where you are not meeting or are exceeding the importance of this value in your life and an asterisk where you feel you meet your values (Diagram 4).

Diagram 4

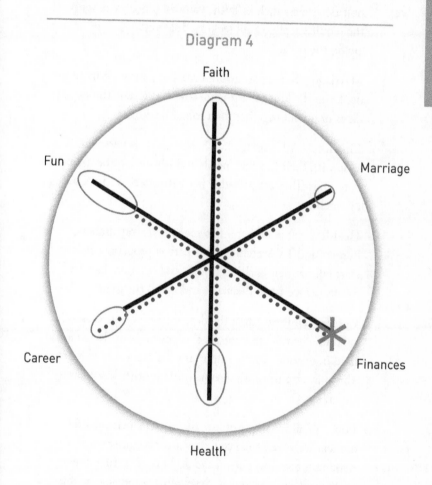

In this example the following aspects are apparent:

▶ **Faith**   This person probably has a solid faith, yet is aware that there are numerous areas they need to improve on. Point to remember: generally speaking, with 'super large'/ holistic aspects such as 'faith', you will probably never meet the requirement you are seeking. That's okay as long as you are on the path.

▶ **Marriage**   Some good work here, but a little bit more to do. Drop the kids off at the in-laws and restart the weekly dates or go out together for a romantic dinner.

▶ **Finances**   All is on track. Chances are this person is in tune with their financial needs and is meeting their regular outgoings. They are probably budgeting well and not going into debt.

▶ **Health**   Not good here. Too many takeaway dinners, burgers and TV-watching. This person probably needs to start taking their health seriously and eat more balanced meals, reduce fat in their diet and get to the gym.

▶ **Career**   Unfortunately, the dotted line far outreaches the solid line here — that means this person is working far too hard in relation to how important their career is to them. This may also be causing some of their other key areas to suffer.

▶ **Fun**   While a couple of key areas in this person's life are relatively well balanced, they are struggling with making it fun. This person should look at cutting down on their career and look at developing some new hobbies and interests (preferably involving some sort of physical activity).

This powerful exercise provides the foundation required to move forward with a solid grounding of who you are, what is important to you and how successful you are in these key areas in your life right now. The outcome of this exercise will change on an almost daily basis, so remember to regularly complete the COMPASS Life Clock, giving you a visual understanding of you and your success.

P
A
R
T

O
N
E

COMPASS Life Clock Exercise

Reflection

How do you feel about this exercise? Happy or sad? Thrilled or disappointed?

....

What are the key areas you feel you are doing well in?

....

....

What are the key areas you need to improve?

....

....

Part Two

Examples of the 1% Principle in your life, work and business

If you're not happy with the way things are in your life, you are the only one who can take responsibility and start making changes.

Personal goals

If you're not happy with your life or your circumstances, you are the only one who can take responsibility and start changing it. What are you waiting for? Follow the 1% Principle today.

Finance

- Set up an automatic payment of $30 a week towards your retirement.

- Commit to assessing all your bank balances and financial agreements.

- Ensure all your insurance policies are up to date.

- Ask your boss for a raise.

- Start a formal savings plan for a larger goal.

- Use price comparison websites to find the cheapest option when buying a medium- or large-sized item. (I did this recently when buying a fridge and found a $200 price difference.)

- Streamline your bill-paying. Set up direct debits for common household bills.

- Start a pocket money/'sanity money' account, so you can indulge in treats without blowing the family budget.

- Challenge yourself to save $10 today.

- Make your own lunch and take it to work rather than buying overpriced (and unhealthy) café or deli food.

▶ Figure out the cheapest way to get to work (including public transport, bicycle, walking and so on) and commit yourself to taking the journey to see what it is like.

▶ Explore a new money-making opportunity that could generate between $50 and $100 a week.

▶ Keep all your receipts for a week and find out exactly where your money is going. Analyse your findings and look to cut back where necessary.

▶ Shop online. You can get practically everything online now, and it also means you won't be tempted to get all the 'little extras' that over time stack up.

▶ Ensure you or your significant other is aware of your current financial situation. Even though this may be stressful, it will reduce ongoing financial pressure in your relationship over the long term.

▶ Think of what you want in terms of the 'big picture', instead of what you think you must have right now. Most things we desire in life are not needs, they are wants.

▶ Take 10 minutes to review your main credit card and bank accounts. Make certain that all charges are accurate and review any purchases you may regret later.

▶ Buy things that will last longer than it takes to finance them.

▶ Do a personal asset stocktake and streamline your life. Do you need three TVs and six laptops for a family of four? We can live a lot more cheaply once we realise that we do not need a lot of the stuff we think we need.

▶ Remember that with financial freedom comes peace of mind. Money problems are often the cause of other difficulties, including those with our health, well-being and relationships with others.

Health

- Get a professional health assessment from your doctor.

- Check your fitness level at a local gym.

- Go for a 10-minute walk around the block.

- Go for one week without fizzy drinks (soda) or alcohol.

- Don't get takeaways tonight, but eat a green salad instead.

- Learn how to do CPR.

- Take half a teaspoon less of sugar in your coffee or tea today.

- Go without butter or margarine for a day.

- Try a new food you have never eaten before and see if you like it.

- Do 10 press-ups and 10 stomach curls.

- Take a serious look at your grocery shopping list, and see if you can cut back on less healthy items, replacing them with alternatives that are good for you, such as oranges instead of cookies.

- Buy some seeds and start a vegetable garden.

- Review your health insurance, and make sure you are fully covered.

- Go to bed half an hour earlier to ensure you get the sleep your body needs.

- Spend time outside in the sun absorbing valuable vitamin D — but avoid sunburn!

- Turn your alarm off on the weekend and make sure you are getting enough sleep.

▶ Do some research on the type of food you are eating. Look for an excess of salt or sugar and see how many preservatives are included.

▶ Try to eat only raw foods (no processed meals) for one week.

▶ Drink eight glasses of water today. When you're dehydrated, you'll have far less energy and get less done.

▶ Ask yourself if there is an area in your life that you are struggling with. This could be mental, physical, emotional or spiritual. Ask someone you care about today for the help and support you need.

Personal development

▶ Read the first three pages of a personal development book you may have been putting off reading.

▶ Dig out some old motivational CDs and listen to one of them.

▶ Commit to trying some local night courses and develop a new skill.

▶ Think about one thing you can do today to be more efficient in your business and working life. Plan your week ahead. Build time for planning into your week.

▶ Create good habits and try to understand the things that cause you to procrastinate and be disorganised.

▶ Think of one thing you have always wanted to study just for enjoyment's sake. Is there a night or online class where you can study it?

▶ Learn how to change a tyre or check the oil in your car.

▶ Find an old hobby or interest you were passionate about in the past and rediscover it today.

► Learn how to set your DVD/Blu-ray/TV recorder.

► Set up a home wireless network.

► Spend 10 minutes reading motivational quotes on the Internet.

► Watch 10 minutes of a motivational speaker on YouTube.

► Reassess your contact with people who have negative attitudes.

► Download three podcasts on a subject you enjoy, and listen to them on the way to work.

► Think of ways to better utilise your commuting time. This could include learning a new language via MP3 or CD.

► Think of a fact that's always confused you. Jump on the Internet and find out the answer.

► Start today towards breaking an old and destructive habit. Break the stages down into small parts then, bit by bit, work steadily towards removing this habit from your life.

► Ask a close and trusted friend to give you some honest and fair feedback about yourself. Perhaps they can follow the Toastmasters formula of C-R-C: giving one or two commendations, one or two recommendations, and a final commendation. After the feedback, analyse what they said, and if you feel it's appropriate, apply it to your life.

► Identify an area where you are struggling in your life and commit to take one small step towards getting unstuck.

Career

▶ Update your résumé/CV with some of your recent achievements. These can include examples such as:

- ~ Being awarded further responsibility such as acting manager or acting second-in-charge
- ~ Coaching or mentoring new staff who join the company
- ~ Setting up more efficient systems or processes
- ~ Detailing any positive references or emails from clients or team members
- ~ Special projects you may have led or taken part in
- ~ Position promotions
- ~ Involvement in any committees or positions of leadership (such as Social Committee chair or Health and Safety spokesperson)
- ~ Exceeding set sales targets
- ~ Increasing market share or generating repeat business
- ~ Introducing key clients to your company
- ~ Any high grades you gained during recent studies
- ~ Scholarships gained during studies
- ~ Winning sales awards
- ~ Developing new promotional/marketing ideas
- ~ Assisting in reducing customer complaints
- ~ Managing any major suppliers
- ~ Taking part in any major relocation projects
- ~ Organising any events/conferences
- ~ Meeting or exceeding performance targets
- ~ Purchasing of any goods/services in your business
- ~ Budget responsibility
- ~ Staff/team leadership responsibility

~ Systems, software and hardware experience

~ Voluntary or unpaid work

~ Articles, papers or features published in any magazines, journals or books

~ Presenting any topics at conferences

~ Completing any public speaking

▶ Find out about further training you can do to improve your 'employability'.

▶ Find an efficient and cost-effective way to improve a system or process in your department.

▶ Do a survey online and find out what people with jobs similar to you are being paid in the market.

▶ For 10 minutes think about what you want to be doing for work in 10 years' time. Write this down and start to plan how you can make this dream a reality.

▶ Think about how you can be seen as a leader in your industry. What can you do today to start this vision and make it a reality?

▶ Think of three things that you love about your job.

▶ Tell a friendly co-worker that you genuinely enjoy working with them.

▶ Start a blog about your professional area of expertise. Over time you will develop a following and be seen as a key person in your industry. However, remember to ensure you do not breach any confidentiality or privacy issues and get an okay from your manager, if required.

▶ Sharpen up all your online profiles (including LinkedIn, Twitter and Facebook), making sure you come across professionally.

▶ Review your business wardrobe and make sure the image you present matches the professional appearance that is required of you in your job.

▶ Imagine you could have your time over again — what would you like to do for your career?

▶ Clean up your desk and rearrange your furniture so it's more efficient.

▶ Add some colour to your office. Make the environment where you work pleasant.

▶ When you make a decision in your job, ask, 'If I owned the business, would I do this?'

▶ Jump headfirst into change, whether it's new ways of doing things, new offices or new teams. Take time to learn new software, take a tour of a new office facility, or introduce yourself to a new co-worker. The more quickly you get used to new things, the more quickly they will become familiar to you. Also, your boss will be happy and use you as a leader to model change for others.

Marriage/partner

▶ Leave a note saying 'I love you' somewhere your partner will stumble across it during their day or send them a loving email.

▶ Give your partner a genuine compliment today that they have never heard from you before. For example, 'I really like your dress style' or 'You look great in that top'.

▶ Have an honest, fair and open discussion about the main thing you argue about in your relationship. (For example, money, sex or children.) What is one thing you could each do to make this problem less of a struggle in your relationship?

▶ Lie down on the bed and spend one minute looking into each other's eyes without saying anything. Finish with a cuddle.

▶ Say something positive to your partner. Research shows that happy couples employ a five to one ration of positive to negative comments.

▶ Ask your partner what they were like as a little kid. What were their favourite secret places, what pets did they have and what were their best holidays?

▶ Think of an area of life your partner has been struggling in. Give them a genuine compliment and tell them how proud you are of them.

▶ Think about a time when something went wrong between the two of you. Ask yourself, 'What could I have done differently? What could we have done differently? What is it we can learn from this?' Talk to your partner about it, starting with what *you* could have done differently.

▶ Cook a meal together. Either work together on one meal, or take turns making an entrée each, while the other person talks and sips wine.

▶ Make your partner a surprise breakfast with all the trimmings.

▶ Pack your partner a gourmet lunch to take to work. Slip in a note saying you love them.

▶ Next time your partner mentions an appointment they are going to (for example, a meeting at work, lunch with a friend or catching up with a family member) make a note and remember to ask them how it went.

▶ Keep a little gift hidden away so you can surprise your partner when they have had a bad day.

▶ Copy and paste the lyrics from your favourite love song into an email and send it to your partner.

▶ Think about something you've both wanted to do together and find a DVD or website that shows you how to do it. Plan a date night around watching it together.

▶ Instead of watching TV, read a story out loud to each other or have a game of cards.

▶ Put on music you both like and dance in your living room.

▶ Complete Gary Chapman's 'Five Love Languages' test (see 5lovelanguages.com), and determine how you and your partner like to give and receive love.

Children

▶ Set up a regular board game night once a week.

▶ Think of a 'tradition' you can start in your family.

▶ Tell your children about your ancestral history.

▶ Organise one-on-one time with each of your children this week.

▶ Take time out to stop and say 'yes', rather than 'no' once in a while. You won't remember the report you were writing in a year's time, but your kids will remember the walk you took them on.

▶ Introduce your children to a skill you are good at. This could be fishing, painting, gardening or working with computers.

▶ Create a secret code for 'I love you'. Use this secret code in public as much as possible.

▶ Put a weatherproof, bench-style storage box outside for the kids' toys.

▶ Learn how to build a fire and a waterproof shelter with your children.

▶ Take time to find a passion both you and your children share.

▶ Do some household chores together as a family. Not only are you teaching them some valuable life skills but you get an opportunity to talk with them about their day.

▶ Move the kids' cereal boxes, bowls and cups to a low shelf so they can reach them.

▶ Attend as many school functions (including plays and sports events) as possible. They are only young once and they will remember whether you were there or not.

▶ Organise an exciting overnight hike in the bush for you and your kids.

▶ Take your kids to a local 'grassroots' rugby game.

▶ Camp out in your lounge and watch some nature documentaries.

▶ Build and fly a kite together in the local park.

▶ Tell your children about the emergency number, and why they shouldn't misuse it.

▶ Make up your own private handshake.

▶ Practise a fire or earthquake drill at home.

▶ Tuck your kids into bed and tell them you are proud of them.

▶ Teach your kids a new skill or sport today.

▶ Talk to your children about a far-off country and the people who live there. Go online and find 10 fun facts about the country, including the colour of the flag, the language spoken and the capital city.

▶ If your children's bedroom is a mess, divide the area into six squares and get them to 'deep tidy' (including vacuuming) each section over six days.

Family

▶ Do a first-aid course and become competent in a family emergency.

▶ Book a surprise dinner for the family for no particular reason. Invite some of your nearest and dearest friends to enjoy the celebrations.

▶ For four days a week, limit your family's total TV, Facebook and YouTube use to one hour per day. Use the time you would normally spend on these things for some fun family activities.

▶ Once you manage to do this, cut out TV and the Internet altogether for two or three days per week.

▶ Do a stocktake of your possessions and sell the items you don't use on online auctions. Use the money generated from the sales for a large family treat or go somewhere new on a family trip.

▶ Plant a tree together.

▶ Go through all your family photos that are on your PC and back them up on another hard drive. You do not want to lose them!

▶ Make a wish-list of sunny and rainy day activities so you don't waste precious weekend time figuring out what to do.

▶ Call your parents or grandparents. Sometimes a 10-minute phone call is all they need to feel loved.

▶ Have regular dinners at the dining room table. This is a great way to get the family together and find out where each other is 'at'.

▶ Bake cookies and ice them together as a family.

Extended family

▶ Contact a long-lost (or near and ignored) relative to just say hi.

▶ Send an email and photos to a relative overseas.

▶ Spend some time on the Internet researching your family history.

▶ Find out if your family has a coat of arms or any interesting history.

▶ Find an interest, area or hobby you and your wider family are interested in, and use that as a way to connect more deeply with them.

Friends

▶ Phone a different friend every day for a week just to catch up and say hi.

▶ Organise to have coffee with a friend you have lost touch with.

▶ Think of all the ways you can support, encourage or bless a friend today.

▶ Organise to go to the movies or a play with a friend.

▶ Cull your Facebook friends back to only those who actually mean something to you.

▶ Make a list of your friends' birthdays and give them a call to congratulate them on the day.

▶ Be there for a friend going through a rough patch, and see if you can help in any way today.

▶ Offer to babysit for a couple who have not had an opportunity to have a night out without their kids.

▶ Host a dinner party once a month, inviting different friends every time.

▶ Jump onto Facebook for 20 minutes and reconnect with some key friends you have lost touch with.

▶ Organise a trip away for you and a couple of close friends for the weekend.

▶ Challenge a friend to a game of tennis or golf.

▶ Reach out to someone new today and establish the basis of a new friendship.

▶ Don't be a problem-solver when a friend just wants you to be a listener.

▶ Send a text to a friend out of the blue, wishing them a great day. This will guarantee they have a smile on their face and know that someone is thinking of them.

Other people

▶ Find a way to make someone feel good about themselves today.

▶ Write a hand-written thank-you note and give it to someone who gave you good service today.

▶ Give someone a genuine compliment for a job well done.

▶ Pay for someone else's lunch today, without them realising it was you.

Faith/spirituality

▶ Pray deeply and without distraction for just two minutes.

▶ Spend 10 minutes reading the Bible or a book by a faith-based author.

- Download a spiritual development app and commit to using it regularly for one week.

- Celebrate your religious events throughout the year wholeheartedly.

- Pray together with a family member or friend. If you're comfortable, discuss and share what you pray about.

- Share a personal testimony of how you were blessed in a particular situation.

- Do some research on your faith (e.g. church history).

- Find an online course based on building your faith and knowledge.

- Spend five minutes praying for your family and your community.

- Think of a way you can positively and practically share your faith with someone today.

Lifestyle

- Find a way to more equally distribute your work-life balance.

- Ask your boss about working virtually from home for one day a week.

- Research passive income ideas and talk with friends who have been successful in this area.

- Start a small part-time business with a maximum initial investment of no more than $100. Create your own free (yet professional) website through an organisation like wix.com.

- Set a goal of generating $10 profit in the first week. Set a goal of generating $20 profit in the second week. Keep going until you have a business generating $100 profit per week.

▶ Look at ways to delegate work to others, or outsource your services to organisations like freelancer.com or odesk.com.

▶ Be disciplined in turning off your work phone and don't answer any emails over the weekend.

▶ Plan your next holiday away today.

▶ Start putting a regular amount away for your holiday, and aim to go on your trip with it paid in full.

Joy/happiness

▶ Write down up to 10 things that you enjoy. For example, spending time with family, going to the movies, exercising at the gym or learning a new language.

▶ Take time to reflect on the last 12 months. What were the joys and successes? What were the disappointments and failures? How can you move forward in the next 12 months?

▶ Assess ways to include more of the things you enjoy in your weekly or monthly lifestyle. Spend some time thinking about what connects you to 'you'.

▶ Think of a time when you felt really alive. What were you doing and how can you capture that feeling again?

▶ Think of a novel or book you have always wanted to read and get it out from the library.

▶ Listen to a new music style that you have not tuned in to before.

▶ Start writing a journal or diary. You will be amazed how therapeutic this can be.

▶ Start writing a blog about something you are passionate about. It could be your family, gardening or birdwatching.

▶ Once you have 20 blog entries, create an e-book and send it to your family and friends.

▶ Once you have 100 blog entries, compile all of them into a second, larger, e-book. Get honest feedback from family and friends, and if it is of publishable quality, sell it online through a shop like amazon.com.

▶ Take stock to see if you are sabotaging yourself in your words today. Understand that what we say to ourselves determines who we are, more than what others could ever say or do to us.

▶ Learn to ignore things that aren't important in your life or don't affect you directly. We live in a world of information overload, celebrity gossip and 24-hour access. Choose to not worry about things that do not have a personal impact on your life.

▶ Go somewhere alone and just 'hang out with yourself'. Listen to the sounds, feel the breeze and focus on enjoying the time with just you.

▶ Research a new hairstyle and see what would suit you.

▶ Do one good deed today and don't tell anyone about it.

▶ Go to a neighbourhood in your town you've never explored before. Try a new restaurant or café and see if you can find a hidden gem.

▶ Buy some flowers and put them around your home or office. They're an instant mood-brightener.

▶ Plan a big party with all the people you have ever wanted together in one big room.

▶ Think of a favourite memory. When you are stressed out, remembering a great memory can relax your mind. And it just might make you smile too.

▶ Give yourself a gift. It might be a week on a cruise, or a day off at home. Whatever you decide on doing, enjoy it with every ounce of energy and appreciation in you.

▶ Take the time today and every day to commit yourself to appreciating everything you have. Start counting your blessings towards happiness.

▶ Remember that no one is in charge of your happiness except you.

▶ Before you get up in the morning, visualise how your perfect day would look. How do you want that day to pan out?

▶ Surround yourself with happy people. It's easy to begin to think negatively when you are surrounded by people who think that way. Conversely, if you are around people who are happy, their emotional state will be infectious.

▶ Learn to laugh at the little things and be amused by your mistakes and failures. Also be thankful that you learned your lesson and won't mess up like that again.

▶ Learn some funny jokes and sleight of hand tricks to entertain your family and friends.

▶ Wake up early and remind yourself how refreshing it is to watch the sun rise.

▶ Do something spontaneous today. It doesn't have to be crazy, mad or dangerous, just step outside your normal schedule and throw responsibility to the wind.

▶ Make a choice to not over-dramatise life by inflating small setbacks into life-threatening catastrophes. This habit makes mountains out of molehills and places you under extra pressure and stress that only causes more issues.

▶ Stop being a perfectionist today. Having a high attention to detail and doing the best job you can is vital to your success; however, perfectionism will destroy all your pleasure and send you in search of what can never be attained.

Community

▶ Think of one way you can assist a community organisation today or this week. Do you know of someone in need in your community? How can you lend a hand? You grow by giving and helping others. It can change you and help you in ways you never expected.

▶ Find and attend a festival in your local area that you would not normally go to.

▶ Every day over the next two weeks, introduce yourself to a new neighbour near your house. Start to develop some local networks and look to see how you can work together and support each other in a meaningful way.

▶ Find some volunteer opportunities through local churches, clubs or groups. Sign up and assist those who need your help!

▶ Be a good neighbour. Be considerate so your noise doesn't bother those around you.

▶ Pick a cause close to your heart and get involved. You don't have to quit your job and dive in headfirst, just get involved on some level and do what you can, when you can. Go slightly beyond your comfort zone, but don't overextend yourself.

▶ Try to make at least three people smile today.

▶ Say goodbye to people who tell you to forget your dreams.

▶ Find a way to introduce yourself to a person you have seen around but don't know well within your community.

▶ Help out and support a local event such as a fun run or a parade.

▶ Think about what you are recycling and make sure everything ends up in the right place.

▶ Reuse old bottles, bags or anything in your house instead of throwing them out and buying them again.

Challenges

▶ Visit a local group and help a community need.

▶ Write down five things you would like to do this year.

▶ Start by taking a practical step towards one of the goals above.

▶ Think of one thing you have always wished to know more about. This could be boating, classical history, mathematics or a language. Find out about a local or online course in your subject of choice and enrol in the next intake.

▶ Set a challenge to do something today you have never done before.

▶ Look at a way you can improve your speaking and communication skills. Research joining your local Toastmasters.

▶ Keep a journal about your dreams, desires and the new life you are creating.

▶ Start a weekly challenge. It could be to lose weight, learn a language, run a certain distance or grow a garden. Check your progress every day.

▶ Research and join a new group. You will meet a new bunch of people who you may develop lifelong friendships with.

Time management/personal efficiency

▶ Think of one thing you can do today to be more efficient in your home life.

▶ Set your alarm clock for 15 minutes earlier and spend this time planning what you want to achieve.

▶ Research new software and online tools that will make you more efficient and organised in your daily life. For example, Gmail, Google Drive, DropBox, online calendars, to-do lists or personal finance software.

▶ Get on Google Maps and see if you can find a faster way to work or to somewhere else you go regularly.

▶ Accept you make mistakes. Take some time out to forgive yourself for the poor decisions you may have made.

▶ Give an object you don't use any more to someone in need. This could be an old suitcase, a pram, or a barbecue.

▶ Commit to reading an entire book in the next week.

▶ Arrange any appointments you've been putting off. Seeing the dentist may not be a fun task, but it will mean you don't have to spend thousands of dollars on dental work and possible reconstruction later on.

▶ Take a quick nap and recharge. Napping is an excellent way to improve your stamina, especially if you have a late night planned.

▶ Whenever you run across anything empty, ripped, the wrong size or never used, immediately toss it in the trash or give it to a charity.

▶ Set up contingency plans. For example, a spare set of car/house keys, a second deodorant, or another way to get kids to school.

▶ Use those cool decorative keys to make it easier to know which key is which (especially at night, in the rain …).

▶ Leave a torch, pen and paper, cellphone charger and $10 change in the car.

▶ Check your car has all the tools you need to change a tyre. You don't want to find you are missing the jack at 2 a.m.

▶ Free up glove box space by putting the owner's manual in the passenger seat back pocket.

▶ Place an emergency box in the car boot. Be sure to include an umbrella, a first-aid kit, a plastic raincoat, scissors, a black marker, duct tape, paper towels, plastic bags and extra children's clothes.

▶ Take an extra business shirt or blouse to work and leave it there as a spare.

▶ Put a small bag for rubbish in your car.

▶ Tidy one drawer a day.

▶ When you adjust your clocks for daylight saving, go through your cupboards and throw out your expired medicine, sunscreen and food. Also check your smoke detectors.

▶ When you load the dishwasher, put all the forks in one slot, all the knives in another slot, etc. This way it will be super-fast to unload the dishwasher.

▶ Do things outside standard hours. Buy your groceries and go to the gym when few others are there. Do normal tasks during off-peak times and you will save hundreds of hours per annum.

▶ Measure and commit to memory the width of your outstretched fingers and the length of your middle finger.

Next time you need to measure a small distance and a ruler is not nearby, you will be able to approximate it more precisely.

▶ Memorise something every day. Not only will this ensure your brain and memory stay sharp, it will make you sound smart in front of your friends when you quote Mark Twain and Ernest Hemingway.

▶ Take a class in speed reading. Speed reading helps you to quickly analyse data and skim through information to find key themes and concepts.

▶ Remember names. You may go into business with or even marry this person you're meeting for the first time, if you make a good impression.

▶ Consider your to-do list. Is it overwhelming you? Eliminate all but the absolute essential tasks and rewrite your list, making it more manageable.

▶ Inaction is the only true failure. If you don't take action, you fail by default and will not learn from the experience. Doing something new today is better than doing nothing!

▶ Have a food basket in your fridge that contains meat, jam, chutney, cheese and other things that can be used to make a quick lunch.

Business goals

Finance

▶ Think of one way to reduce business expenses by 1% that you can apply today. Consider remote work arrangements for you and your team.

▶ Look into sharing an office with another business.

▶ Assess your telecommunications spend and analyse whether cheaper alternatives are available.

▶ Switch to Internet-based phone services. Just remember to check the call quality and ensure it's at the standard you require.

▶ Implement paperless systems and try not to print things. Printer ink/toner is more expensive by weight than champagne.

▶ Buy recycled printer cartridges rather than new.

▶ Practise energy-saving behaviours by turning off office lights and computers at the end of the day.

▶ Look for free software alternatives, rather than more expensive commercial options.

▶ When you travel, try to book ahead as far as possible to get the best deals.

▶ Form a buying alliance with another business or a trade association for bulk purchasing discounts.

▶ Seek at least three bids on everything major you purchase. On a recent exercise I completed, I saved 50% between the highest and lowest quotes, without loss of quality. Ask suppliers if they give discounts for early payment.

Human resources

▶ Think of an encouraging way you can motivate a member of your team today.

▶ Assess ways to recruit talented new employees through staff and industry networks.

▶ Design an advertising template to streamline your recruitment processes.

▶ Design an easy-to-use job description template to more easily create position descriptions.

▶ Come up with a quick way you can improve your team's morale today.

▶ Determine three things your staff works for. Is it money? Status? Lifestyle? Find out by asking some of your closest team members and get more in touch with what drives them at work.

▶ Take a genuine interest in your team and plot their birthdays in your diary.

▶ Assess job titles for top performers. It costs nothing to improve someone's title but may mean a great deal to them personally and may change the way they are perceived in the workplace and wider industry.

▶ Ensure that your top performers know you have a solid career progression plan for them, so they can develop through your business in the future. Many employees leave businesses because they feel they have hit a 'glass ceiling' and can't progress any further.

▶ Organise fun and exciting social engagements which bring the team together. These can be both on-site (casual dress day) and off-site (trip to a local sporting event).

▶ Start up company sports teams. These are a great way to bring the IT, HR, sales, finance and customer services departments together.

Supply chain/logistics

▶ Assess the products and services your company uses, and see if any other suppliers can provide the same products/services for a cheaper cost.

▶ Negotiate cheaper rates with your current suppliers for the products and services you are using.

Sales

▶ Contact current clients to ask for more business.

▶ Think of one new initiative you can put in place to increase business income by 1% this week.

▶ Identify one current product or service your business offers that you can propose to a current client who is not using this solution.

▶ Don't just network for networking's sake. Go out there and develop strong relationships and friends. It's easy to spot the fakes, and people will refer you more often if they genuinely feel you like them.

▶ If you want to present products and services that are of value to your client, you have to ask questions. Ask the right questions and they will tell you what they want and how they need to be sold.

▶ Selling does not mean convincing your client or overcoming objections. Instead, see yourself as your customer's partner in solving their problem.

▶ Go through your client base and complete the '80/20' exercise. Find the 20% of clients that cause the most problems and discreetly drop them. With the new time you have available, concentrate on generating new, quality business leads.

▶ Don't be put off by gatekeepers. Ensure you are talking to the real decision-makers.

Marketing

▶ Spend half an hour researching your competitors' marketing and see what works for them.

▶ Assess what is best practice advertising and marketing in your industry. Research a target demographic, tailoring a new advertising campaign specifically for their needs.

▶ Go on the Internet and check out similar companies operating in different international markets. What do they offer that you do not? What can you add to your products and services that would be of benefit to your customers?

▶ Ask for referrals from current clients who are your 'fans'. By telling others what they've gained from using your business, your sources can encourage others to use your products or services.

Benchmarking against other organisations

▶ Research competitors' systems and tools they use in their day-to-day business. You will be surprised what you can find online.

▶ Look to see if any systems they are using can benefit your business.

▶ Identify a new target market or industry you can research.

Strategic planning

▶ Break down your organisation into between five to eight key areas. (For example, sales, human resources, finance, marketing, administration, etc.). For each of these key areas, brainstorm what these areas will look like in 10 years' time if the organisation is very successful.

▶ Brainstorm what these areas will look like in five years' time if the organisation is very successful.

▶ Brainstorm what these areas will look like in one year's time if the organisation is very successful.

▶ Set tangible short-, medium- and long-term goals for each of the key areas above. This process will allow you to quickly develop a framework for each of these areas, as well as set signposts to determine your success on an ongoing basis.

Information technology

▶ Assess cloud options for your computing systems.

▶ Set up off-site back-up options, even if you regularly back up your information to a local hard drive. If there is a fire or theft, you could lose everything.

▶ Assess other less traditional options for your work. Is a tablet more suitable and efficient for your work if you primarily use only email?

▶ Take 20 minutes to read about latest technology updates in recent blogs and magazines. Assess how these apply specifically to your industry.

Health and safety

▶ Identify a way you can introduce a new health and safety concept to your workforce this week.

▶ Set up a 'bright ideas' box to highlight major health and safety issues.

▶ Run a fun quiz with prizes, using your company's health and safety handbook as the main reference tool.

▶ Conduct free on-site health screenings for employees like blood pressure and cholesterol screenings.

▶ Encourage healthy eating habits by removing vending machines filled with snacks and beverages with high calories and low nutritional value.

▶ Set safety goals, such as 'six months without a lost time incident'. Reward employees for achieving the goals by taking them to the movies or hosting a company picnic.

Change management

▶ What are some systems/tasks/processes in your organisation that need to be culled?

▶ Spend 20 minutes thinking of a way to positively promote a new project to your staff, rather than just saying 'This is what we are doing so put up with it!'

▶ Create short-term wins and set regular small goals that are easy to achieve.

▶ If things start to go wrong, act quickly and get the process back on track immediately.

▶ Empower people to make decisions at the local operating level.

Performance improvement

▶ Identify one way you can improve the performance of your department by 1% this week.

▶ Now look at how you can do this every week for the next 10 weeks.

▶ Pick a process and ask why it is done this way. After you have asked this question, see if there is a more efficient way to do it. Sometimes organisations do things just because 'that's the way it's always been done', rather than it being the most efficient method.

▶ Think about how you can automate some of the manual processes you currently have in place.

▶ Identify any processes or services that can be outsourced.

Process/systems improvement

▶ Research via the Internet new ways to improve current systems and processes in your workplace.

▶ Ask colleagues and industry association members what tools, resources and systems they use in their businesses. See if you can utilise some of them at your workplace.

Customer services

▶ Look into whether there are special discounts or services you can offer that your competitors don't.

▶ Identify one thing you can do with your next customer to make their day. Find a way to go above and beyond with every single customer interaction today.

▶ Take the time to get to know some of your key customers and, if appropriate, take a genuine personal interest in them.

▶ Could your services be considered premium? Offering special treatment and deals to your customers will help them to feel taken care of, and it's also something they might be willing to pay more for.

▶ Every time you interact with a customer, in person or over the phone, initiate a quick discussion to gauge how they are feeling with your product or service.

▶ Smile when greeting a customer face to face as well as over the telephone (and, yes, they can tell if you are smiling over the telephone!).

▶ Remember the live customer standing in front of you takes precedence over someone who calls on the phone.

▶ Learn to read body language to see if a customer could use some help.

▶ Inspect goods the customer has purchased before bagging it to make sure it's not defective or the wrong size.

▶ Make sure customers receive everything they've paid for before they leave your store.

Event management

▶ For your corporate Christmas party, research how you can save 1% off the total cost, yet provide the same or an even better experience than last year.

▶ What are some innovative corporate gifts you can give to clients that will make you stand out from your competition?

▶ Look to shave 1% off the transport, catering and staffing costs for your next event, without the participants being aware of it.

Quality control and efficiency

▶ Identify a simple way you can improve a small production process and make the manufacturing process 1% more streamlined and efficient.

▶ What is a way you can improve the quality of your product or service by 1% this week?

▶ What is a new tool, white paper or template you can create that you can then give to your clients free of charge?

Part Three

Use the 30 Day Programme
to successfully implement
the 1% Principle in your
life, work and business

Now that you have a good understanding
of how the 1% Principle operates, the
next step is successfully implementing
it on a daily basis.

The 30 Day Programme: developing the 1% Principle into a habit

By now you should have a pretty good understanding of how the 1% Principle operates in the real world. The next stage is successfully implementing it on a day-to-day basis, to develop the 1% Principle from an abstract concept into a regular and enjoyable habit.

Remember:

▶ Fully commit to the 30 Day Programme. It's really simple (it is the 1% Principle after all …), and after three or four weeks the principle will become automatic.

▶ Only do the 1% Principle exercise allocated for that day. Don't try to completely change your life straight away — you have the rest of your life to do that! It is easy to get over-motivated and take on too much, setting yourself up to fail.

▶ Remember to do it. Set up reminders around your home and workspace so you remember to do the exercises each day.

▶ Having an accountability partner will help you supercharge your progress towards your goals. Ask your accountability partner to contact you every day via email, text or phone, to confirm that you completed that day's exercise.

▶ Make it a game. Have fun during the 30 days and challenge yourself to complete all exercises on time and to maximum effect.

▶ Do it for you and you only. If you complete the 1% Principle 30 Day Programme for someone else, you won't get the same results as you will doing it solely for yourself and your personal development.

▶ Reward yourself along the way. This will reinforce positive behaviours and make the 1% Principle habit stronger.

Day 1:
What's your passion?

'The more intensely we feel about an idea or a goal, the more assuredly the idea, buried deep in our subconscious, will direct us along the path to its fulfilment.'
—Earl Nightingale, motivational speaker and author

If you are the sort of person who gets excited on Friday night because the weekend is here, and on Sunday evening dreads going back to work, chances are you are lacking passion in both your work and personal life.

It's easy to get motivated about something you are excited about. Going to a movie you have wanted to see for a long time or having a special dinner with your partner is something that is easy to be excited about. Any hurdle that gets in the way will be brushed aside as you strive to make the movie's start time, or find a park near the restaurant.

Tapping into this passion is an easy way to start achieving your mini-goals. Passion for a goal will drive you on and force you to confront the hurdles and negative thoughts that need to be overcome. You will become incredibly creative in finding ways to move around, under, over or even through the obstacles that block your way.

As author and motivational speaker Anthony Robbins says, 'Passion is the genesis of genius.' Passion helps you to keep the goal first in your mind and gives you the continual drive to carry on, even when things don't go your way.

If you are not sure where your passions lie, ask family and friends the following questions:

- ▶ What am I really good at?
- ▶ What do you think my passions are?
- ▶ What subject makes my eyes light up when I am talking?

After you have these answers, ask yourself:

- ▶ What activities make me forget what time it is?
- ▶ What compliments have others given me recently?
- ▶ If I were instantly qualified to teach any subject in the world, what would I teach?
- ▶ When I'm at the end of my life, what would I regret not doing?
- ▶ What are the three things I have done in my life of which I am most proud?

The answers you get will start to give you an indication of where your passions lie and what things excite you. Passion is the 'petrol in your tank'. The more passion you have for a goal, the further you will go towards achieving it.

Your passion may be in your work, but if it is not (like for most people), it's vital to find something you are passionate about as an outlet for your mental and physical well-being. Understand, of course, that 'passion' needs 'reason' to work alongside it, like two wheels on a bicycle, working in unison, moving you safely on your journey. Too much passion and you tend to throw caution to the wind. Too much reason and you probably won't end up going anywhere.

Today's exercise

Spend some time today making a list of the things that make you excited and which you are passionate about. Once you have these things clear in your mind, you can begin to start living an exciting and rewarding life.

Day 2:
'You miss 100% of the shots you don't take!'

One of the best pieces of advice I ever received was from a poster at my church when I was about 22 years old. We all know the type: one of those traditional motivational posters with some well-meaning phrase designed to get us all excited. While I have seen and enjoyed many such posters, this one instantly changed my perspective on life.

The photo was of an old basketball hoop that hadn't seen a ball aimed at it in many years. Paint was peeling off the backboard, the wall was water-damaged and spiderwebs clung to the forlorn and rusty hoop. Underneath was written: 'OPPORTUNITY'. Then the words that changed my life: 'You miss 100% of the shots you don't take!'

Immediately, I was hit by the incredible truth of the statement. It is so true, and is a recognisable attribute of successful people. Successful people don't give up. They just keep going and going until they get the results they want. On most occasions they're not the most intelligent, the loudest or the bravest. Ninety-nine per cent of the time they are simply the most persistent, pressing on when everyone else has given up.

> 'I have not failed. I've just found 10,000 ways that won't work!'
> —Thomas Edison

Even Edison would have been tempted to stop when failure cursed him again and again. However, he just dusted himself off and tried another approach until he got something that worked.

In today's PlayStation world, it's easy to sit down and be comfortable, yet not go anywhere or achieve anything of value in life. I encourage you today to take some risks, be daring and look a bit of a fool if necessary.

Today belongs to you, but only if you seize it with both hands and have a shot!

Today's exercise

Choose something you have always wanted to do but have not had the confidence to attempt. It might be contacting a publishing house about a book idea, emailing a business about a job opportunity or asking a person you are interested in out on a date. Remember you miss 100% of the shots you don't take.

Day 3:
The power of
visualisation

Both Brian Tracy and Jim Rohn have written: 'All improvement in your life begins with an improvement in your mental pictures.' We are all products of our thoughts, and our attitude is the main determinant of whether we will succeed or fail today.

A great tool to set our attitude on the right track is visualisation. This involves taking the time to picture yourself actively working towards and achieving a particular goal. For example, this may include a difficult dance routine, a job interview or a major client presentation. Stop and think about the environment. What does the room look like? Who is there? How does the first minute of the presentation/event happen? From here start visualising that the event is going really well. How does this make you feel? What is the audience saying about your presentation? What is the feedback you are receiving?

Create in your mind the 'finished product', showing your brain what success in this situation looks and feels like.

Research has shown that you stimulate the same brain regions when you visualise an action as when you actually perform the action. This is an astounding fact, as we can literally fool our brains into thinking something 'is' by visualising it taking place. This can work strongly in your favour when you are thinking about achieving a particular goal.

'Your subconscious mind recognises and acts upon only thoughts which have been well-mixed with emotion or feeling ... You will get no appreciable results until you learn to reach your subconscious mind with thoughts or spoken words which have been well emotionalised with belief.'
—Napoleon Hill, *Think and Grow Rich*

As a professional speaker, I enjoy visualising myself standing in front of audiences and presenting to an excited and enthusiastic group. This gets me in the groove and helps to take some of the edge off prior to a major speech.

A key benefit of visualisation exercises is that they can also help you rehearse and improve the goals you wish to achieve. Before a recent keynote address, I diligently visualised how I would address the audience, what I would be wearing, and so on. During my mental preparation I suddenly came up with a fantastic introduction that had not occurred to me during my normal preparation. This revelation would not have taken place if I had just rehearsed my notes and gone through my PowerPoint slides endless times.

Visualisation is a technique used by professional sportspeople looking to improve their performance by 1%, on many occasions determining the difference between victory and failure. Golfers, boxers, divers and baseball players have all testified as to how visualisation sharpens the senses and improves performance.

At the very least, visualisation provides the following benefits:

▶ It gives you a positive attitude and approach to a goal.

▶ It provides the ability to overcome mental barriers and get a level of mental clarity.

▶ It provides the ability to correct bad habits.

▶ It offers a chance to model best practice.

At the end of the day, who can't benefit from a few of these things in a time of need?

Today's exercise

Think of an area in which you would like to achieve success. It could be meeting your life partner, achieving financial security, or having a particular experience, such as sailing in the South Pacific. Take some time today to visualise the experience, putting your mind's eye in the moment, letting this take you closer to your goal.

P
A
R
T

T
H
R
E
E

'The future you see
is the future you get.'

—Robert G Allen, author

Day 4:
Be optimistic

'A pessimist sees the difficulty in every opportunity; an optimist sees the opportunity in every difficulty.'
—Winston Churchill

Too many people wake up in the morning with a mental chip on their shoulder. It's a 'glass half-empty' mentality that makes days drag and relationships difficult. Negative thoughts are crippling and can easily outweigh any physical handicap a person has. Your attitude determines your altitude — your attitude determines how high you fly in life and how far you travel.

What we believe, we achieve. It's as simple as that! If we believe we deserve success, we subconsciously take on a successful mindset, seeing the upside to situations and correspondingly taking advantage of new opportunities. However, if we feel we are a failure, this belief will work itself into our deepest psychology, and we will have a 'glass half-empty' mindset.

Take a set of golf clubs, for instance. Even if the best golfer in the world tries to hit a ball as far as they can with a putter, the average Sunday golfer can outmatch them with a driver. The size of the golf club in this instance determines the impact it will have on the ball. Therefore the more impact (belief) we have, the further the ball will travel.

It's important we also protect our minds from comparing ourselves to others and their successes. The messages we receive from advertising and media can be fake, with even supermodels having their images airbrushed in PhotoShop to give consumers a completely false sense of reality.

In summary, think about the best in every situation and guard yourself against negative messages we receive both from ourselves and from others.

Today's exercise

Take an area of your life, say a person or a situation that you tend to struggle with in regards to an optimistic attitude, and try to turn the glass from half-empty to half-full. Focus on the 'bright side' and look hard to find that silver lining. You will be surprised by the results.

Day 5: Focus

It's far too easy sometimes to get distracted by the day-to-day monotony of life and therefore not achieve our goals. The phone ringing, the washing in the dryer or the email that has just come in all seem to demand our attention immediately. However, having a strong focus towards achieving a goal is a time-tested way to ensure that that goal is achieved quickly.

Take a magnifying glass, for example. The lens can quickly concentrate the sun's heat and energy and turn a piece of paper into a charred ruin of its former self in a matter of seconds.

When I think of this type of focus, a couple of things come to mind:

1 Focusing on an outcome transfers potential and relatively harmless energy (for example, the sun's rays) into a powerful force, setting the scene for massive change in the short, medium and long term.

2 The magnifying glass works by creating a larger 'virtual image' of the object behind the lens; that is, the object you are looking at is larger than life size. This helps you to gain an understanding of its key properties and structure, rather than just having the view that everyone else sees.

We succeed or fail in our goals according to how much focus we can bring to bear on them. When we have focus, we make time to achieve our goals, even if there is inconvenience or pain, because we know that when we make it to the other side the outcome will be worth it.

'One reason so few of us achieve what we truly want is that we never direct our focus; we never concentrate our power.'
—Anthony Robbins, author, motivational speaker

Today's exercise

What is a goal you can focus on today to bring it that little bit closer to fruition? Turn off the TV, the radio and the PlayStation and set some time to focus on making great headway towards your goals.

Day 6:
Take time out

I have an approach to life that I call 'moment making'. When I was studying towards my degree in psychology, I noticed that people tend to remember their life in 'highlights'. They remember a special birthday, a trip away, or a unique moment that came about randomly. What they don't remember are the 180 Friday nights at the local bar, the 2100-plus hours playing PlayStation or the 10,000 hours of TV they watched over the last three and a half years.

I am not saying that going to the pub or relaxing at home is a bad thing, but it is vital we look back on our years with wonderful memories of a life well lived, not a whole bunch of 'grey' that we can't quite recall.

As my wife and I have two boys, living this principle is even more important. As parents we must actively create moments — that create memories — that build lives! I live in fear of being the father in Harry Chapin's famous song 'Cat's in the Cradle', the story of a father who was too busy to create memories with his son until it was too late.

Many of these moments need not cost a lot of money and can be as simple as camping overnight on the back lawn, having a weekend away at a motel, or getting in your car and discovering a new park, beach or café near your house.

A very wise friend of mine, Pastor Guy Rook, says, 'Be intentional in your living.' We must actively take the time to create these moments, or time will just march on by without anything memorable taking place. My wife Sarah actively organises events throughout the year, ensuring we have things we can look back on and laugh at the fun we had together.

You must actively choose to create a life full of fun and enjoyable memories. The reward is a positive ongoing legacy for you, your family and your friends.

Today's exercise

Plan an exciting event you would like to do this month. It could be taking the family to the movies, going away for a weekend or having a picnic.

'Create moments —
that make memories —
that build lives!'

—Tom O'Neil

Day 7:
Become accountable

I firmly believe that being accountable is one of the most powerful things you can ever learn.

When I gained a publishing contract to write my first book, *Selling Yourself to Employers*, my publishers loved the concept. I was ecstatic and excited about developing my career as a writer. 'However,' my new publisher added as we sat around the negotiation table, 'we really need another eleven thousand words to round the book out, so can you have it to us by this time next month?'

Choking back my surprise, I agreed and then tried to figure out how I could make this happen. Putting together a plan, I hit on a brainwave. I asked my wife to be my accountability partner, asking her to ensure my word target was achieved each day. This worked so well I actually exceeded my goal, and wrote 15,000 words in one month.

As a general rule, it is difficult to get people excited and motivated about a goal. Even worse, it is harder for them to stay motivated. Psychology professor Dr Gail Matthews led an amazing study in which 267 participants from a wide variety of businesses and organisations were divided into five groups.

▶ Group 1 was tasked with thinking about various business-related goals they hoped to achieve within a four-week period.

▶ Groups 2 to 5 were asked to write their goals and then rate their successful accomplishment the same way as Group 1.

▶ Group 3 was also asked to write action targets for each goal.

▶ Group 4 had to both write goals and action targets and share these commitments with a friend.

▶ Group 5 went the furthest by doing all of the above, as well as sending a weekly progress report to a friend.

When the study was completed, Group 1 had accomplished only 43% of their stated goals, while Group 5 were the most successful, with an average 76% of their goals achieved. Staggeringly, those with an accountability partner achieved their goals a whole third more than those who only thought about their goals.

This study proves that being accountable to another person for your results can add real strength to your ability to reach your dreams. However, when you choose your accountability partner(s), I suggest you think long and hard about the best people to ask to take on this important role.

For each of the key areas of life you highlighted for your COMPASS Life Clock, you may wish to have a separate accountability partner. Some people may have more authority in your life than others. For example, your brother may be your 'financial' accountability partner, your sister may be your 'spiritual' accountability partner and your husband or wife may be your 'family' and 'health' accountability partner.

Just remember that whoever you choose needs to be supportive, encouraging, a bit bossy and have your genuine best interests as their focus.

Today's exercise

Think of the people you know who have achieved success in specific areas of their lives; for example, in their marriage, health, career or finances. Make a note to ask them if they would be prepared to act as accountability partners for you in the future.

Day 8:
Be authentic to yourself and create a personal vision

In the world of professional speaking, new members are told again and again to be 'authentic' in their message. On so many occasions, new speakers try to copy other professionals, mimicking their message, style and presentation, and using what seems to be a tried and tested formula, hoping it will lead to their success. The truth is that these people invariably fail, as they are not true to who they are and what they are passionate about.

> 'Don't ask what the world needs. Ask what makes you come alive, and go do it. Because what the world needs is people who have come alive.'
> —Howard Thurman, author, philosopher and theologian

In today's society, we are continually pushed and prodded to conform to someone else's agenda and view of who we should be. Therefore, it's very important to create a personal vision and make a stand for who you are. A personal vision distils and clarifies who you are and what is important to you, allowing you to make quality decisions in your life.

'I was once afraid of people saying, "Who does she think
she is?" Now I have the courage to stand and say, "This is
who I am."'

—Oprah Winfrey

Today's exercise

Project forward to your life in 20 years' time and ask yourself the
following questions:

- ▶ What are some of the key successes I have had over this
  period? (Think especially in relation to your key areas from
  the COMPASS Life Clock exercise.)
- ▶ What are some of the main values I have held during this
  time?
- ▶ What are the things I will not tolerate in my life?
- ▶ What is it I stand for?

Using the information from above, craft your personal vision in,
ideally, no more than three sentences. Make it easy to understand
and remember, ensuring it is a positive reflection of the 'authentic'
you. Once you have your personal vision, print off a copy and pop
it in your wallet or save the text to the splash screen of your phone.

A sample vision for a financial planner might be:

'I am a well-respected business person who has helped thousands
of families get debt-free and understand the need for sound
financial planning.

'I am focused on having integrity in every situation, and my
key values include love, respect, faith, honesty and sincerity.

'As a loving father and husband, our children have been
successful in their chosen areas and my wife and I base our
relationship on mutual trust.'

Once you have written your personal vision, you will be surprised
by how powerful it can be when you reflect on it on a daily basis.

'Dreams give to the soul
what food gives to the body.'

—Robert Lewis

Day 9:
Be persistent

I was recently provided with an excellent example of persistence and the results it can bring. My wife was watching a kids' movie on TV with our two young boys and some very inappropriate and violent advertisements came on about halfway through. Now, Sarah could have done what most people who saw those ads did and just moan to their family and friends. However, Sarah thought she would take a stand about this poor-quality programming. She wrote a considered and well-structured complaint, highlighting the key areas of broadcasting law and where she felt they had been breached.

Sarah systematically approached three different authorities, going higher and higher each time, only to be told at each step it 'wasn't their responsibility'. Finally, the process stalled. By now any rational person would be thinking, 'This is too hard ... Do I stop the fight? Should I not worry about this and just move on?'

Thankfully, this annoying and frustrating process only infuriated my wife more, resulting in her contacting the leading family advocacy group in the country, which culminated in an article in the country's leading Sunday paper. In addition, Sarah contacted our local Member of Parliament who emailed her straight back while visiting another country during an international trade mission.

Due to Sarah's persistence, questions were asked at the highest levels in the land and a commercial advertising law was changed, stopping breaches of this sort.

You know, it is so easy sometimes to feel the fight is just too hard, too frustrating. However, the most successful people in the world have also felt that frustration in demanding situations, but have chosen to rise above it, plotting the next steps to take when all the doors appear closed.

> 'Let me tell you the secret that has led me to my goal. My strength lies solely in my tenacity.'
> —Louis Pasteur, chemist and microbiologist

A lot of the time it's not the fastest, the most intelligent or even the best who succeed. It's the person who stares adversity in the face and just carries on regardless, knowing they will reach their goal one way or another.

Today's exercise

What areas are you being challenged in at the moment? Do you have a wall standing before you that you need to get over, under or around somehow? Write down some active steps you can take this week to break down some of those things that have been holding you back!

Day 10:
Take risks

If aliens landed on earth and read only the front page of a national newspaper, they would see a world of fear, destruction and anxiety. Sadly, we are fed a diet of fear from the media because bad news seems to sell more papers or get more advertising dollars than good news.

When we read papers or watch the news, these fears can take hold in us, then rule our lives, handicapping our ability and desire to try new things and take risks.

> 'The key to success is to focus our conscious mind on things we desire, not things we fear.'
> —Brian Tracy

There are so many reasons for and ways in which we limit our minds and limit our potential. I encourage you to try something new. New can be scary, but new can also be rewarding, fun and memorable. Sample something new and you may actually like it.

Once you get confidence with a small amount of risk, your fear level will start to diminish and you can start to live a life full of joy and freedom. You will start to learn new skills and become more confident in yourself.

Today's exercise

Commit to doing one fun thing you have never done before within the next seven days.

Day 11:
Get organised

One major key in making the 1% Principle work for you is to be organised in all areas of your life.

Symptoms of poor organisation can include missing appointments (both business and family), email overload, or having an unrealistic expectation of what you can achieve within a week. These factors can create more stress in our lives, culminating in a frustrating existence where we feel we never quite measure up to who we should be as a parent, partner and employee.

A simple key to reducing a lot of this frustration is acquiring the skill of organisation. By being organised we have more time and we are more efficient in our management of it. Every minute you spend planning your day will save you five or 10 minutes later on.

Very simple (yet powerful) 1% Principle ways to get organised include:

▶ Take a minute to identify what frustrates you the most and start there.

▶ Spend time in the morning planning your day to maximise your tasks, travel and meetings.

▶ Find a system that suits you. Organisation can only be maintained if it fits into your daily life.

▶ Decide whether you're at your best in the morning or afternoon, then schedule your day accordingly.

▶ Organise your email, documents and paperwork.

▶ Delegate tasks to other teammates and staff.

▶ Manage your banking online.

▶ Set up a diary system that works.

▶ Clear your desk at work once a week.

▶ Set aside tasks that don't require much thought for your low points in the day.

▶ Prepare effectively for meetings and keep to the agenda.

▶ Organise your space.

▶ Make sure you put things back where they belong.

▶ Have a weekly to-do list and diligently work your way through it.

▶ Post-it notes are your friend.

▶ Get plenty of sleep and eat healthily.

▶ Hang up your keys (preferably by the door).

▶ Ask your boss if you can work from home one or two days a week.

▶ Pay your bills on a regular basis.

▶ Know when to say 'when'.

▶ Learn to say 'no'.

▶ Good enough is good enough — procrastination is often a form of perfectionism. Just aim for a little progress every day.

▶ Schedule and delineate specific time for work, home and play.

▶ Understand that your personal and family time should be at least as important as work time.

▶ Organise a drawer that's bothering you. Spend 10 minutes emptying it out. Decide what to keep and arrange it so that similar items are stored together.

▶ Eliminate junk mail immediately.

▶ Make mornings as smooth as possible by planning your wardrobe and meals the night before.

▶ Keep a large family calendar in a central location. Each family member should have their own colour and can be responsible for keeping their information updated.

Today's exercise

Pick a tip from the list above and implement it today.

Make a list of five other ways you can be more organised, and commit to implementing these ideas over the next week.

Day 12:
Work to your
strengths

'Success is achieved by developing our strengths, not by eliminating our weaknesses.'

—Marilyn vos Savant, columnist, author, lecturer

No one is superman or superwoman! We can't be amazing at everything, and it's a good thing this is so.

I believe we spend too much time looking to improve areas we are weak in, rather than developing our God-given strengths to take us to the next level. Looking at highly successful entrepreneurs, scientists, artists, athletes and entertainers shows us that they achieved greatness by focusing on where they are strong, not where they are weak.

Everyone has a natural skill or strength in something. We all have a special gift that we can use to bless ourselves, and others. You may be talented at languages, working with numbers, cartooning, playing the guitar, creative writing, empathy, teaching adults or growing vegetables. Whatever your key strengths are, you must use them to their full potential.

Don't spend too much time looking to be competent at everything. Instead, hire someone who is strong where you are weak, delegate tasks you don't enjoy to others who do enjoy those things and automate repetitive tasks.

Today's exercise

Ask yourself the following questions:

- ▶ What are my strengths and what do I do well? To help you answer this, ask 10 family members and friends to give you honest feedback.

- ▶ What are my weaknesses and what sort of things do I struggle with? Again, ask your family and friends for their honest thoughts.

- ▶ What sort of job would I love to do right now if I could walk into any role?

- ▶ What things do I do that seem almost effortless?

- ▶ What things do I do where time just seems to fly by?

- ▶ What activities make me happy and make me smile?

- ▶ What things would I do with no promise of financial gain, but because they're fun, enjoyable and interesting?

Look through your answers to these questions to find common themes. These are likely to be the areas of your natural strengths, aptitude, skills and talent. They are the areas of greatest potential for you. Research 10 ways this week to develop these skills and take you to the next level.

Day 13:
Craft consistency

'Simply let your "Yes" be "Yes" and your "No", "No".'
—Matthew 5:37

Consistency is a learned skill. We all know people who have let us down when they said they would support us, or promised to be there, then didn't show up just at our time of need. Those experiences hurt, and many of us are left emotionally scarred by empty promises and assurances that weren't delivered.

To have a strong standing among your peers, crafting a reputation of consistency is one of the most powerful things you can do. Letting your 'yes' be known as a 'yes', and your 'no' be known as a 'no' sets a standard for others to follow.

You will be seen and trusted as reliable and dependable, opening up further opportunities at work and in your personal life. People know that when they ask you a question they will get an honest and fair answer, or receive an assurance that something can or can't happen.

However, be supportive, caring and compassionate in how you deliver your consistency. Being a jerk consistently does not work! A straightforward answer to a problem may be the most efficient way to deliver the news, but taking some time to phrase something more diplomatically can be just as important on many occasions.

At the end of the day, be known by your family, friends and co-workers as a person who is reliable and trustworthy: someone they can come to when they have a problem and need support.

Today's exercise

Think of some examples of where you have been unreliable or not dependable in what you have done. If you had the opportunity to go through those same situations again, what would you do differently? Moving into the future, what are some practical ways in which you can be known as a reliable, honest and consistent person to those around you?

Day 14:
What is success
to you?

An area of life I am almost constantly challenged with is what success means to me. Driving to and from the city on my commute to and from work, it's impossible not to be influenced by the hundreds of messages written by advertisers desperate to get me to own a new car, have whiter teeth, buy a better DVD player ... Of course, so many things that are of critical importance today are a fleeting memory tomorrow.

I have a good friend who is an immense success financially. Building a commercial real estate empire from the ground up, he recently bought a Ferrari, trading in his Porsche. However, his trade-off is a lot of time away from his family in a job he is not passionate about. In some ways he has become a 'rat race refugee', as business speaker Rachel Prosser calls it. While your career may be important to you right now, no one on their deathbed said, 'I wish I'd spent more time at the office.'

Another friend worked hard, both during the week in his own company as well as in the evenings and weekends, building a large motorhome for his family. His plan was to travel around the country as a family once the motorhome was finished, investing time in getting to know his family better.

After three years of only seeing her husband in between when he got home and when he retreated to the garage, his wife left him permanently, taking the kids with her. The heartbreak for my friend was that, in his mind, he had been doing this for his family.

He realised too late that he was not taking the immediate needs of his family into account.

Take a personal stocktake of what success means to you. It's vital that you are not swayed by others' interpretations of success, and you only take into account what is important to you.

What is success to you? A loving family? A nice car? A big boat? A job you enjoy? A career that challenges you? Moving up the corporate ladder? Further learning?

Choose today to define what success is to you, then work hard to make this an ongoing reality.

> 'Living a life that matters does not happen by accident. It's not a matter of circumstance but of choice. Choose to live a life that matters!'
>
> —*Los Angeles Watts Times* reporter Michael Josephson, in an article on the life and legacy of Rosa Parks

Today's exercise

Write down your personal definition of success. Look at the following areas for inspiration:

- Faith
- Friends
- Family
- Health
- Financial security
- Leisure/fun
- Career
- Challenges

Ask five of your friends to define what success means to them. How are your ideas similar to and different from your friends'? What are the good things you can take from your friends' definitions and include in your life? What are some aspects from your friends' definitions that you are not prepared to sacrifice in your life?

Day 15: Getting and keeping momentum

'I have been impressed with the urgency of doing. Knowing is not enough; we must apply. Being willing is not enough; we must do.'

—Leonardo da Vinci

Getting and keeping momentum towards your goals is a vital part of being successful. Without momentum, your interest can quickly wane, and you may end up back where you started, but more despondent than ever.

A good way to gain a lot of momentum initially then keep it up is to use my MMC Motivation Model: momentum–motivation–celebration.

Firstly, you need momentum to start the process. This is the hardest part when no one but you believes in your goal, resources are scarce and time is precious. However, once you push through this first stage and start to gain progress, the next level is motivation. You now have things under way and it is easier to keep the motivation up and work towards your goal. The initial push has been made and you are starting to see the fruits of your labour. Others are now starting to buy into your success and you are starting to get a few supporters along the way.

The third stage is celebration. As you move closer towards your goal, have mini-celebrations at each milestone. This keeps you excited about the task, and ensures you circle back into the first stage (momentum) with a positive focus.

Today's exercise

Think about the MMC Motivation Model in relation to a project you are currently working on or a goal you are working towards. How motivated are you at present and what level of momentum do you currently have?

Is there a mini-celebration that is overdue where you can demonstrate your progress to a family member or friend who will be supportive?

Think of a way you can stimulate your interest in the project, increase your motivation and gain the critical momentum you need to achieve your goal.

Day 16:
Become a better
communicator

'Communication — the human connection — is the key
to personal and career success.'

—Paul J Meyer, founder of Success Motivation Institute

To be a success in any area of your life, you have to get people on
your side and have them agree with your point of view. Whether
it's a sales transaction, business deal or marriage proposal, getting
a person to say 'yes' is strongly linked to your communication
skills.

I am not talking about 'manipulation'. This is the opposite of
communication in that you are imposing your will on a person.

God gave us two ears and one mouth for a reason. Active
listening is so important in allowing us to understand what
other person are saying and what their needs are, rather than us
jumping the gun and providing a solution that they may not need
or want. Non-verbal communication techniques such as positive
eye contact, posture, gestures and listening can play a huge part
in emphasising a verbal or written message. Most psychological
studies say that non-verbal communication accounts for around
60 to 70% of all meaning in a conversation.

Keys to successful communication include the following:

▶ Don't talk, listen. When somebody else is talking, listen to
what they are saying and do not interrupt.

▶ Focus on the other person and try to understand the message behind the message, not just what they are saying.

▶ Listen to the tone and non-verbal communication.

▶ Stay focused, absorb the information given, and find a way to follow up with a question relevant to the subject.

▶ Use open-ended questions. Open-ended questions that provide a detailed answer are one of the best ways to engage a person in communication.

▶ Be genuine in your interest. Even the least astute person is conditioned to understand whether or not you are genuinely interested in them and their needs. People will look forward to interacting with you because they feel happier and uplifted doing so.

▶ Maintain eye contact and look the speaker in the eye. This helps the other person understand that you are there and listening.

▶ Practise your communication and interpersonal skills. These can be improved and organisations such as Toastmasters can give you some excellent tools to allow you to take your communication to the next level.

Your ability to communicate effectively with other people will be the single largest determinant towards your success.

Today's exercise

Take the challenge today to engage a person in conversation for more than 10 minutes. During this time try to find out:

▶ Their favourite colour

► The name of their first pet

► The movie they enjoyed the most

Setting and attempting little 1% challenges like this one will allow you to quickly improve the skills you need to develop a positive rapport with others across almost all situations.

Day 17:
Take joy in the
small things

The key to having the 1% Principle become highly effective in your life is to take joy in the small things that you come across every day.

Mindfulness is a technique of tuning into life, slowing down, observing and appreciating what's around you. Take time out to live in the moment (not in the past or in the future). Remember that 'present' has three distinct meanings: 'here', 'now' and 'gift'.

Another way to take joy in the small things is to simplify your life. Too many of us are racing to check our emails and texts, as well as meeting deadlines others have set for us. Simplifying your life does not mean living in a tent at the bottom of a field, however. It can be as simple as:

- ▶ Diarising some time just for yourself during the day.

- ▶ Turning off the phone and email after work.

- ▶ Spending time with family and friends who give you energy, rather than those who take energy from you.

- ▶ Learning to say no and delegating more.

- ▶ Limiting your exposure to media and advertising.

- ▶ Learning to live more frugally.

- ▶ Learning what 'enough' is.

Today's exercise

▶ What are practical ways you can slow down and practise mindfulness?

▶ Ask: 'Will this simplify my life?' If the answer is no, then reconsider.

▶ Spend just one minute today appreciating a small thing you have not noticed before. It could be a flag waving in the distance, a breath of wind across your face or savouring the taste of coffee early in the morning. Savour it, treasure it and be grateful for it.

PART THREE

Day 18:
Practise gratitude
in all you do

One symptom of modern living in Western society is that we have so much yet value it so little. This is commonly known as 'affluenza', a condition that comes from keeping up with the Joneses, advertising overload, debt, anxiety and the fevered pursuit of more and more!

In their book *Affluenza: When Too Much Is Never Enough* Clive Hamilton and Richard Denniss argue that affluenza causes over-consumption, consumer debt, overwork and harm to the environment. This in turn manifests itself in a wide range of antisocial ways, including drug and alcohol abuse.

On the other hand, having a spirit of gratitude helps us understand how blessed we are every day.

Doing work with my church in India and the Philippines, I was witness to a wide range of living conditions, from five-star hotels, to parents and children living rough on the street. This experience started to change my heart towards the things I wanted and expected in my life. When I got back home, I became less of a consumer and started to focus more on quality of life, rather than quantity of life.

Twenty years later I have thankfully managed to retain some of this gratitude in my regular life, and look every day to be thankful to God for what I have been given and what I have worked hard for.

As well as this, the art of practising gratitude helps us have a caring and compassionate mindset. It ensures we are more patient with ourselves and others, and it allows us the freedom to not chase a newer car, bigger boat or more expensive house we simply cannot afford.

Once you grasp the concept of practising daily gratitude, be prepared to give back to your family, friends and community in money and time. Remember that success unshared is failure.

> 'Gratitude is not only the greatest of virtues, but the parent of all others.'
>
> —Cicero, Roman philosopher

Today's exercise

Find 10 things to be genuinely grateful about today. Share these things with someone close to you and see if you can pass on your new grateful spirit to them.

PART THREE

'The healthiest of all human
emotions is gratitude.'

—Zig Ziglar, author, salesman,
motivational speaker

Day 19:
Practise self-discipline

'Self-discipline is the bridge between goals and accomplishment.'

—Jim Rohn, author, motivational speaker

Those who have achieved sustainable success are the ones who can truly master self-discipline over themselves. In every area of our lives, those who put in that 1% more effort will be the ones who rise to the top. Whether it's in relationships, faith, health or your career, the hundreds of little disciplined decisions are the ones that matter the most.

While someone may be proud they didn't pig out at the work function buffet, they also need to take into account the chocolate bar and two fizzy drinks (sodas) they consume on a daily basis. Someone else may be thrilled they resisted the temptation to buy a $200 shirt which was on sale, but the $20 a day spending habit on other goods more than adds up to this over 11 days.

It's the small things that matter, and making sure you are disciplined enough to plug the small leaks will allow you to more wisely manage your money, friendships and health over the long term.

'It was character that got us out of bed, commitment that moved us into action, and discipline that enabled us to follow through.'

—Zig Ziglar

Today's exercise

- ▶ What is an area of your life or career you are struggling with in regards to self-discipline?

- ▶ What is just one thing you can do today to start moving forward in this area?

- ▶ Commit to making this step today, and follow it through over the next seven days.

Day 20:
Opportunity — COMPASS Goal Achievement Programme

In Part One, we started the first part of the COMPASS Goal Achievement Programme — **Consider**. In this exercise, you completed the COMPASS Life Clock, assessing what is important in your life, and finding out where you are right now in the key areas of your life.

The second part of the COMPASS programme is **Opportunity**. If you had the opportunity to do anything in life, what would it be?

In the 2007 movie *The Bucket List*, Jack Nicholson and Morgan Freeman play two terminally ill men who escape from a cancer ward and head off on a wild road trip with a wish-list of things to complete before they die. Of course, we shouldn't have to wait to be in this situation to write a list of things we would like to achieve before we 'shuffle off this mortal coil'.

Today's exercise

The goal in this exercise is to develop our own bucket list and expand our mind to understand what we can actually achieve. What are some of the things you would like to achieve for you, your family and your career before you kick the bucket?

Imagine if money was not an issue and there was nothing to

hold you back. What are the things you would like to do, have, learn or achieve before you die?

By doing this exercise, you will discover some of the key things that matter to you. These may include faith, family, the outdoors, excitement or travel. For example:

- ▶ Learn to salsa.
- ▶ Teach a family member a new skill.
- ▶ Write a book on something you are passionate about.
- ▶ Have a romantic dinner — in Paris.
- ▶ Run the New York City Marathon.
- ▶ Get an advanced qualification.
- ▶ Spend a week visiting the Louvre museum.
- ▶ Visit the Taj Mahal.
- ▶ Learn how to play the saxophone.
- ▶ Drive across Route 66 on a Harley-Davidson.
- ▶ Spend a week in each of Europe's capital cities.
- ▶ Go on a round-the-world cruise.
- ▶ Grow and eat your own vegetables.
- ▶ Buy a 35-foot fishing launch.

Write your bucket list, and dream big!

Day 21:
Map — COMPASS
Goal Achievement
Programme

Map out your goals and make SMARTA plans for your life. George Doran changed goal setting for good when he wrote in his 1981 *Management Review* article 'There's a S.M.A.R.T. way to write management goals and objectives.' In his article he outlined what was to become the world's most powerful goal-setting mantra. SMART was a mnemonic to be used as a guide when setting objectives: the goals should be Specific, Measurable, Attainable, Realistic and Time-sensitive.

In my COMPASS Goal Achievement Programme, I have added an 'A' to the end of the SMART goals plan, for Accountability.

Setting SMARTA goals

Goals help us achieve our dreams, but if they are not SMARTA, they are just dreams. A well-written goal should have the following components:

- ▶ **Specific** A specific goal has a much greater chance of being accomplished than a general goal.

- ▶ **Measurable** Establish concrete criteria for measuring progress towards the attainment of each goal you set.

▶ **Attainable**   You can attain almost any goal you set when you plan your steps wisely and establish a time frame that allows you to carry out those steps.

▶ **Relevant**   Your goals must be relevant to your life. Therefore, remember that each goal can be refined or even deleted as your life changes.

▶ **Time-sensitive**   A goal should be grounded within a time frame. Without a time frame, there's no sense of urgency.

▶ **Accountable**   According to Dr Gail Matthews, you have a higher chance of achieving a goal if you are accountable to someone else.

Today's exercise

Take each of your key areas from your COMPASS Life Clock and examine them thoroughly. For each of your key areas, develop some short-, medium- and long-term goals using SMARTA.

Short-term goals should be completed within the next 12 months. Medium-term goals are one to five years away and long-term goals are over six years distant. Medium- and long-term goals may be more flexible and less specific due to their far-off nature.

Put the name of the person you are accountable to in brackets beside each goal. Make sure they know they are your accountability partner, and that they can quiz you at any time in regards to your progress.

If you are struggling to define goals for some of your areas, you may wish to start with your long-term goals, then work back, defining how to achieve them over the short and medium term.

Remember, the difference between a dream and a goal is a piece of paper!

Sample goals in your 'Finances' section may include the following:

Short-term

▶ Save $50 per week for 20 weeks for a holiday to Fiji (Tim).

▶ Save $40 per week for 30 weeks for a child's braces (Lisa).

Medium-term

▶ Save $9000 for a friend's overseas wedding in two years' time (Ngaire).

▶ Pay off credit card balance of $6000 within three years (Carl).

▶ Finish paying off car loan of $4000 within the next two years (Lee).

Long-term

▶ Save $25,000 for a new boat within five years (Nigel).

▶ Pay off mortgage of $250,000 within 20 years (Gail).

▶ Gain passive income of $1000 per week within eight years (Sam).

This is a large exercise which will take a few hours to complete, so get started today. Commit to completing this exercise within the next two weeks.

Day 22:
Proceed — COMPASS Goal Achievement Programme

'The secret of getting ahead is getting started.'
—Mark Twain

Start taking active steps towards your goals and **proceed**. Many people work hard at writing their goals, but too often these same goals quickly end up in the bottom drawer and are never heard of again.

In the 100 metres race, most of the time the race is won at the start. In the case of Usain Bolt's 100 metres final victory at the 2012 Olympics, he won by 0.12 of a second. This is half the time it takes to blink your eye. A great start was pivotal to him crossing the line ahead of his competition.

Goals are like that: it is vital to start well. Starting well increases your motivation, then gives you the momentum to keep going until you cross the line. With a poor start, we think to ourselves, 'I am not a goal-setter' or 'This goal-setting stuff is not for me!' With a great start your self-talk is quite different: 'I have achieved some small goals, so I can and will go on to completion!'

> 'Once the first step is taken, the momentum builds up that propels us to go with the flow, enabling us to have an ordered focus and be productive at the same time.'
>
> —Prashad Navaranjan, author, motivational speaker

Today's exercise

Write down 10 things that you can do this week in order to start actively achieving some of the goals you set down yesterday. These may include:

▶ Finding out exactly (to the last cent) what is owed on your credit card.

▶ Finding out how many more months you have until your mortgage is up for renewal.

▶ Going for that first walk or run of one kilometre (remember to start small — if you try to achieve massive goals immediately, you may get discouraged and stop working towards them).

▶ Buying a board game to play on the new 'family games night'.

▶ Swallowing your pride and phoning a relative or friend you may have lost contact with over a disagreement.

▶ Going to the supermarket and buying fruit and vegetables.

▶ Committing to a daily reading plan to read the Bible in one year.

▶ Registering in a local fun run.

▶ Getting a night-class syllabus and registering for a course in a skill you want to develop (e.g. safe boating, welding, scrapbooking).

▶ Buying a personal development book and reading the first chapter.

Write down 10 things you can do this month to start actively achieving some of the goals you have set down.

Day 23:
Assess — COMPASS
Goal Achievement
Programme

You must regularly **assess** your goals to ensure you are actively taking consistent steps towards their achievement. For example, if you want to save $12,000 to buy a boat in 12 months' time, you should have $6000 saved within six months. If you want to have a family games night once a week, think about how many you have had in the past six months.

This gives you the opportunity to see how you are progressing against your set timelines and performance targets. Once again, SMARTA goals are excellent as they give you a framework against which to measure your achievement.

Remember that as you progress through life, circumstances change. You may get married or you may relocate to a new city. Chances are that over time goals which made perfect sense 10 years ago are no longer important in your life. For example, owning a classic car collection may not be so important now if you have just had triplets. This time of reflection and assessment gives you the opportunity to set new goals more in line with your current lifestyle.

Today's exercise

Set up regular times throughout the year to revisit your goals. For example, this may be the first Saturday of every month. Ask yourself the following questions for each goal as you assess them:

- ▶ Is this goal still important for me? Should I delete it instead?
- ▶ How am I progressing towards achieving this goal?
- ▶ What do I need to do to ensure I achieve this goal within my timeline?
- ▶ Do I need to develop another goal in this area?

P
A
R
T

T
H
R
E
E

Day 24:
Score — COMPASS
Goal Achievement
Programme

'You just can't beat the person who never gives up.'
—Babe Ruth, baseball great

Too many people start the goal-setting process all fired up, but at some stage they become discouraged and then give up. Remember, to be a success in your life you must **score** — complete what you aimed to do.

It is easy to lose track and get disheartened when redundancy strikes, your car breaks down or your finances hit a brick wall. Sadly, this is what most people do in their career, family life, spiritual life and so on.

The pattern is the same:

1 Trials and frustrations hit.

2 This causes us to temporarily lose our focus.

3 We then fall behind our goals.

4 We finally give up completely.

However, you must be committed to the end and keep your eye on the prize. This is also where your accountability partner will be invaluable. Make sure you are in regular contact with them, especially if you are going through a challenging period. They need to be kept informed so they support and inspire you to keep the motivation going, and get you to the next level.

Life is too short to not give it all you have, so remember to score and work hard towards completing your goals.

Today's exercise

What are areas of your life you have struggled with and given up on? What are some short-term SMARTA goals you can set today to get these areas back on track?

Day 25:
Success — COMPASS Goal Achievement Programme

It's a great feeling when you actively put in place a goal and then methodically work towards achieving it. Think of some way to celebrate your **success** in proportion to the size of the goal you have achieved. For example, if you have successfully paid off your mortgage, go on an overseas trip as a celebration to toast your achievement.

My wife and I have a strong success motivator for our goal of raising two young boys into adulthood. From the birth of our second boy Joseph in 2005, we have put aside $20 every week to take a six-month holiday across Europe when they leave home (around 2030 …). While that is currently a long way off, Sarah and I still get excited when we think of cruising through canals in Venice and flipping coins into the Trevi Fountain in Rome.

Today's exercise

Write down five things you would like to do to celebrate completing some of the larger goals you have set for yourself.

Day 26:
Become resilient and happy with change

The definition of the word 'resilient' is to be 'capable of withstanding shock without permanent deformation or rupture' and 'tending to recover from or adjust easily to misfortune or change'.

The ability to be successful in your life depends to a large part on your resilience and how happy you are with change. Those who struggle in both areas find it difficult to let go of old ways and are afraid to move into the future.

Change can be good and, on many occasions, change is going to happen with or without our permission. Therefore, it's up to us to proactively practise resilience on a daily basis and get ready to accept change when it comes.

> 'In order to succeed, people need a sense of self-efficacy (the ability to believe in their ability to achieve a set task), to struggle together with resilience to meet the inevitable obstacles and inequities of life.'
> —Albert Bandura, psychologist, Stanford University

Today's exercise

What is an area of change or pressure you are going through at the moment? What is one thing you can do today to begin to craft the skill of resilience and become more comfortable with change in this situation?

Day 27:
Be a loving family member and friend

'And now these three remain: faith, hope and love. But the greatest of these is love.'
—1 Corinthians 13:13

Picture this: You are 100 years old, and are relaxing in a wicker chair overlooking the sea on a beautiful cloudless day. Looking back on your life, you mentally go through the people who meant the most to you and had the most impact on the person you became. As you relax further into your chair, you realise these are the people who you should have trusted more, spent more time with and forgave more often.

As we go through life, we either accumulate emotional baggage through others' words and actions, or we actively look to cast off these things and move forward in grace and peace.

Some disagreements seem to be so important and powerful at the time, but less so in hindsight. The person who cultures love, respect and forgiveness in their heart and in their actions will be the one who lives a fuller and more meaningful life.

Today's exercise

Who is a family member or friend who you have had a minor disagreement with? Text or phone that person today to reconnect, without bringing up your grievance. Genuinely show forgiveness and patience, remembering how grateful you will be that you did this exercise and re-established this relationship when you look back in the future.

P
A
R
T

T
H
R
E
E

Day 28:
Who am I?
Who do I want to be?

'Know thyself.'

—Ancient Greek aphorism

Some of the most important questions you will ever ask yourself are 'Who am I?' and 'Who do I want to be?' The sad fact is that many people, with their busy lives and desire to watch TV rather than plan their future, never take the time to truly evaluate who they are and where they are going in their lives.

However, the fact that you are reading this separates you from millions of others who prefer to cruise through life with no direction or plan. Knowing who you are and what you stand for is pivotal to moving forward successfully.

When we choose the type of life we want to live, then take active steps towards achieving this life, that's when great things begin to happen and we start making a positive mark on our career, our family and our community.

Remember to always be fundamentally engaged and honest with yourself.

'Destiny is not a matter of chance; it is a matter of choice. It is not a thing to be waited for; it is a thing to be achieved.'

—William Jennings Bryan, three-time US presidential candidate

Today's exercise

Head up a page with the words 'Who am I?' Halfway down the page write the heading 'Who do I want to be?'

Under the first heading detail all the things that come into your mind about your role in your family and your community, your strengths, your weaknesses, your attributes, your faith and so on. For example, some of my list reads:

'Christian. Father. Husband. Procrastinator. Hard worker. Poor at attention to detail. Big thinker. Not fit. Board member. Member of my church. Entrepreneur. Joyful. Blessed. Excited. Excitable. Rash. Trusting. Proactive. Not too good with practical things.'

Remember this list is to both celebrate who you are as much as to find areas where you can improve your life.

Once you have written down a list of what you believe makes you the person you are today, look at any negatives and detail under the second heading the attributes, skills and strengths you would like to have in the future. My list includes:

'Wise. Think before I act. Balanced. Healthy. Fit. Good at attention to detail. Calm. Measured. Charismatic. Inspiring trust. Great with practical things.'

You may want to take this list with you throughout the day so you can include things as you go. Once you have completed this exercise, take some time out to:

- ▶ Celebrate the positive things that make you happy with who you are.

- ▶ Assess the areas you are not so happy with.

- ▶ Reflect on the qualities and attributes you want to develop in the future.

▶ Start planning some steps for how to get there.

If you are comfortable with sharing this list with someone you care about, I suggest you do. However, understand that some people may suggest attributes you may not agree with! Sharing this information with someone you trust makes the process more real and brings in a degree of accountability.

Day 29:
What to do when
your goals go wrong

A little while ago I had the opportunity to see a small goal of mine fail completely.

A few years ago my wife, our two boys (aged three and five at the time) and I moved to a farm just outside New Zealand's largest city, Auckland. On arriving in our new country paradise, my wife convinced the family to get four hens so we could have fresh eggs every day. All went well for a number of months, and we had fried eggs, poached eggs, scrambled eggs and omelettes regularly for a limited investment in chicken feed.

However, one day Sarah went out to the chicken coop and discovered that my hen 'Henny' (yes, we named them all) had died overnight. All were sad in the household, but Sarah and I thought it would be a great opportunity to demonstrate to the boys the circle of life and death.

'Let's have a funeral,' I stated, and went off to dig a grave for our beloved former pet and egg manufacturer. After 10 minutes of digging, all was ready. Sarah led the boys along the path to where Henny's grave lay, with Tim (the oldest) holding the hen by its feet. We gathered around the grave and the boys, Sarah and I said a prayer each, thanking the Lord for the short but enjoyable time we had had with our chicken. At the signal, I instructed Tim to drop Henny into the grave, but as he did so, it slipped from his hands and landed on the bottom of the grave feet first, staring back up at us as if it was alive.

While this was quite unnerving, the best was yet to come. I thought the easiest way to lay Henny on her side was to prod her a bit with my spade. However, as I shifted her over, the blade of the spade caught underneath her wing, and compressed her lungs, forcing the chicken's last breath back through her vocal cords.

'Brrrooork' the dead chicken squawked!

There was silence for a second or two then the sound of screaming children and heavy running as they scampered away from the seemingly undead zombie chicken. A few minutes later Sarah and I managed to find the boys and bring them back to the site to finish the ceremony, convincing them that Henny really was dead.

Later on, I reflected on this event in line with my speciality as a goals expert and three things came to mind regarding times when your goals don't quite go according to plan:

1 If other people don't share your vision or outcome of the goal you set, they may not complete their tasks quite to the standard you expect. Had I put the hen in the grave myself, all would have gone according to plan. Therefore remember to have the key elements of your goal under your direct control if possible. If you can't do this, try to get the other people involved to share your passion for achieving this task. This may also involve including them in some of the payoff at the end.

2 Things don't always go according to plan ... How hard is it to bury a chicken, for example? When things get in the road of us achieving our goals (such as a change in your financial situation, sickness suffered by you or a loved one or the loss of your job), stop and take some time out to set up contingency plans and readjust your goal time frames, if necessary. Things will always get in the way of us achieving the goals we set, and the bigger the goal, the higher the chance it will be disrupted in some way.

3 Have a sense of humour. The boys ran off in fear and Sarah and I just stared at each other in shock. Life's full of zombie chicken moments, and we can choose to freak out, get angry or just look at each other, smile and try to find the funny side.

Remember to keep moving forward, and watch out for those zombie chickens.

Today's exercise

Think about something you tried recently that wasn't successful. What made the goal fall apart, and what could you do next time to achieve a more positive outcome? Can the goal be resurrected by extending the time frame or putting more financial resources towards it?

Day 30:
The incredible power
of just asking

I am constantly amazed that one of the biggest keys to success is so simple yet so powerful. I truly believe that one of the most potent tools we have at our disposal is the ability to 'just ask'.

I am not talking about asking the universe to help me with some major life issue, but tangible things like 'Can I have a raise?', 'Would you like to go out for a coffee?' or 'Can I write an article in your new book?'

Randy Pausch, former Carnegie Mellon professor and inspirational speaker, in his book *The Last Lecture* explained the power of 'just asking'. While waiting with his father to go on the monorail at Disneyland, his dad commented that it would be great to sit at the front, but then added: 'They would never let us in the driver's cabin.' Randy (a former 'imagineer' at Disney Studios) said he knew a secret to sitting in the front and would demonstrate it to his father. Going up to the driver, he asked, 'Can we sit in the front with you, please?' 'Of course,' the driver said, and away they went ...

Just asking is one of the most underused yet most powerful tools we have at our disposal. I know in my life I have had some great successes when I just asked politely for what I was seeking. If you don't ask, the answer is always 'no'. However, if you just ask, and the answer is 'yes', it could change your life.

Another example of 'just asking' is when I set my goal on being published in the world's bestselling career guide, *What Color Is*

Your Parachute? I had developed a tool in my résumé-writing business cv.co.nz to help clients identify their career and personal achievements and sell themselves professionally to employers.

What was the worst thing that could happen if I sent my key career development tool to the author, Richard Bolles, and he didn't like it? Nothing ... Therefore, I spent a lot of time and put together a professional proposal, outlining why I felt my work could add value to his book. With great trepidation I sent it away.

After a month I hadn't heard anything, so I respectfully emailed him again. Next month no reply, so I sent another email to him. This carried on for nine months until, one sunny morning, I received an email from the author saying he really liked the tool and wanted to include it in his guide.

From those few emails I sent, my work in *What Color Is Your Parachute?* has now been translated into 11 languages and published around the world.

Remember: Most people regret what they did *not* do in life, rather than what they did do. Therefore, I encourage you to think of something to ask for today — and go for it! The results could change your life forever.

Today's exercise

Over the last 30 days, you have been looking at ways to incrementally improve your life by 1% every day. Today, think of an action that would leverage your progress, then find a person who could assist in this area and ask for their help. If they say no, keep asking until you get someone who says yes.

Conclusion: Applying the 1% Principle every day

'For want of a nail the shoe was lost.
For want of a shoe the horse was lost.
For want of a horse the rider was lost.
For want of a rider the message was lost.
For want of a message the battle was lost.
For want of a battle the kingdom was lost.
And all for the want of a horseshoe nail.'
—Medieval proverb

Time and again we see that the little things matter. Imagine if the rider in the above proverb was proactive, prepared and had packed an extra nail in his field kit. The battle would have been won and the kingdom saved.

At the end of the day, only you and your state of mind will determine whether you will be a success or not. It has nothing to do with your parents, your education, wealth or socioeconomic situation. You either want to reach the next level of performance in your family, business and personal development, or you just sit on the couch in your comfort zone, watching while other people get busy doing what you deep down wish you could achieve.

Only you can choose to take the decision to make that 1% improvement today.

After completing the 30-day challenge, I recommend you now

focus every day on improving your life, and the lives of those around you, by 1%.

Turn it into a habit and a lifestyle choice. Every day think of opportunities to reach just that little bit higher, or move forward just that little bit further.

After grasping the true power of the 1% Principle, you will start to apply it many times a day in almost every situation. Once this happens, your potential becomes unlimited.

Go forward and be great!

God bless
Tom O'Neil

Award-winning motivational and inspirational speaking

Through his dynamic and fun presentation style, Tom will teach you and your team tools to put in place effective strategies to reach your full potential. Visit tomoneil.com/speaking.html

- *The 1% Principle — Improving your performance TODAY!* Small daily improvement leads to massive medium-term change. 'What is one thing I can do today to improve my life by 1%?' (Keynote, workshop and breakout options.)

- *Goal getting — Not goal setting* Core principles for effective goal planning and achievement in your life and organisation. Introduction to Tom's COMPASS Goal Achievement Programme. (Keynote, workshop and breakout options.)

- *Just do it* Ensure your team takes accountability for its decision-making and is motivated to get things achieved today, not tomorrow. (Keynote, workshop and breakout options.)

- *Tailored speaking events to meet your needs* Contact Tom direct to discuss tailored messages for your organisation. These can be addressed to a specific need or a wider area of interest within the realm of personal/corporate goal development and personal leadership.

One-on-one COMPASS Goal Achievement Programme coaching and mentoring

COMPASS
Goal Achievement
Programme©

Work one-on-one with Tom and unleash your potential across every area of your life. You will actively set and map out the professional and personal life you desire, as well as detail practical and tangible ways to achieve your goals.

Individualised one-on-one coaching will ensure you move forward with confidence over the short, medium and long term. Visit tomoneil.com/Products.html

Find out more at www.AchievementExpert.com

Phone: +64 9 235 8484 • Email: info@tomoneil.com